浙江省普通高校"十三五"新形态教材

国际贸易系列教材

FOREIGN TRADE CORRESPONDENCE

外贸函电

王 雪 / 主编

ZHEJIANG UNIVERSITY PRESS
浙江大学出版社
·杭州·

图书在版编目（CIP）数据

外贸函电：英文 / 王雪主编. — 杭州：浙江大学
出版社，2022.9（2025.1重印）

ISBN 978-7-308-22968-5

Ⅰ.①外… Ⅱ.①王… Ⅲ.①对外贸易—英语—电报
信函–写作–高等学校–教材 Ⅳ.①F75

中国版本图书馆CIP数据核字(2022)第154208号

外贸函电
WAIMAO HANDIAN
王　雪　主编

责任编辑	李　晨
责任校对	郑成业
封面设计	春天书装
出版发行	浙江大学出版社
	（杭州市天目山路148号　邮政编码310007）
	（网址：http://www.zjupress.com）
排　版	杭州朝曦图文设计有限公司
印　刷	杭州高腾印务有限公司
开　本	787mm×1092mm　1/16
印　张	13.75
字　数	356千
版印次	2022年9月第1版　2025年1月第2次印刷
书　号	ISBN 978-7-308-22968-5
定　价	45.00元

浙江大学出版社市场运营中心联系方式：0571—88925591；http://zjdxcbs.tmall.com

前 言
Preface

　　党的二十大报告明确提出"教育、科技、人才是全面建设社会主义现代化国家的基础性、战略性支撑"。[①]要坚持教育优先发展,建设教育强国,坚持为党育人,为国育才,全面提高人才自主培养质量。报告还提出要"加强教材建设和管理","推进教育数字化,建设全民终身学习的学习型社会、学习型大国"。[②]本书是浙江省普通高校"十三五"新形态教材,是集教材的体系性和市场畅销书的可读性与实用性于一体的立体化特色教材。 本教材适用面广泛,既可供高校国际贸易、电子商务、市场营销、国际商务、物流管理等经管类专业教学授课选用,也适用于各高校的外贸类通识选修课的教学与自主学习,对于有意应聘外经贸相关工作和自我提升的校内外群体均有裨益。

　　随着传统外贸与电子商务的快速融合发展,外贸实践中函电的形式和内容有了极大的变化。本教材主编在自己编写并已试行3年的教学讲义的基础上进行增补和完善,秉持内容实用、语言适用、编排易用的特色化原则,期望打造出一本畅销书式的教材。

　　本教材主要特色如下:

　　1. 内容的实用性。本书各章样函素材均选自近年的外贸实际案例,且每章都有基于同一主题下不同业务场景的多样化的实战信函展示和分析。读者可在具体任务中学习函电写作技巧,形成外贸思维,实现外贸函电写作知识与外贸业务知识的融合与无缝衔接,同时也能够举一反三,应对和解决外贸业务工作中的实际问题。

　　2. 语言的适用性。本书参考英语语言学习特点和新时代函电的表意变

[①] 习近平,高举中国特色社会主义伟大旗帜 为全面建设社会主义现代化国家而团结奋斗——在中国共产党第二十次全国代表大会上的报告 [R]. 北京:人民出版社,2022:33.

[②] 习近平,高举中国特色社会主义伟大旗帜 为全面建设社会主义现代化国家而团结奋斗——在中国共产党第二十次全国代表大会上的报告 [R]. 北京:人民出版社,2022:34.

化,对于实际业务案例中的原始案例进行二次加工,既保证了案例函电语言的简洁性和地道性,又兼顾了教材语言的规范性和专业性。

3. 编排的易用性。全书主要内容共10章,包括8个专题和2个系列案例,整体内容适度。每个专题对应一章,每章内容既连贯,又相对独立,便于读者根据自身需求自选不同专题有针对性地学习。为适应更广泛的学习群体,本书讲解与分析以中文为主。同时,在浙江省高校在线开放课程共享平台(http://www.zjooc.cn)开设有定位于通识类课程的外贸函电线上课程。由主编本人讲授的外贸函电为浙江省线上一流课程。

本书10章对应的专题分别是:

第1章,商务电邮基本知识专题——去繁就简,带你入门;

第2章,业务开发专题——零起点,教你速成;

第3章,询盘专题——分类处理,区别对待;

第4章,发盘与报价专题——细致准确,体现专业;

第5章,交易细节沟通专题——坚持底线,持续沟通;

第6章,订单与合同专题——注重时效,合理回复;

第7章,履约专题——换位思考,妥善处理;

第8章,索赔与售后专题——保持沟通,着眼未来;

第9章,系列案例一:以退为进、适度引导、突破低价、达成交易;

第10章,系列案例二:关注高端、有效沟通、循序渐进、高价成交。

第1章以问题引导,第2—8章均采用外贸业务场景任务驱动法和项目教学法来引导读者学习和帮助教师安排教学。第9—10章精选了两个不同业务背景的实战案例,引导读者置身于仿真业务情境中,通过对一系列连贯的真实往来函电的深度剖析,来逐一了解不同阶段邮件写作的操作细节和跟踪客户的技巧,从而精准把握客户需求,运用邮件解决问题,达成交易。

本教材各章均配有对应的视频讲解、数字化练习答案及教学用PPT。

本教材由王雪担任主编,对教材总体进行设计并负责各主要章节内容的编写和全书审定。乔雯担任副主编,李麒参与编写,二人主要负责对部分章节内容进行修改和加工,以及拓展资源部分和练习的编写等。杨家瑞在书稿后期处理和数字化材料补充中也助力良多。在教材编写过程中,编者参考了一些外贸公司的真实案例,同时借鉴了部分教材和市场畅销书,在此向他们表示感谢。

由于作者水平有限,教材中若有不妥和错误之处,恳请读者批评指正。

王 雪

2025年1月于宁波

目 录
Contents

Chapter 1

Fundamentals of Business E-mail

商务电邮基本知识专题
——去繁就简，带你入门

学习目标

··

☆知识目标

✓了解商务电邮"1＋4"组成部分的内容及操作建议；

✓掌握商务电邮齐头式细节要求和正文框架结构。

☆能力目标

✓能够解释商务电邮的3C原则；

✓能够参与讨论商务电邮的细节要求；

✓能够比较商务电邮和信函的结构异同；

✓能够就外贸人的技能要求阐述自己的观点。

1.1 Introduction 知识介绍

沟通在外贸业务中起着非常重要的作用,外贸企业与外界沟通的主要方式是外贸商务函电。外贸函电主要指进出口贸易环节中产生的信函往来,从业务开发阶段的建交函、询价信,到交易磋商阶段的报价信和还盘函,以及商讨关于装运、包装、支付、保险等交易细节的往来邮件,还有订单信、售后函等,这些都是外贸函电的内容。

以前的外贸函电,主要是信函或传真的形式。随着时代的发展,电子邮件替代了原来的书信和传真,成为商务书面沟通的主要方式。同时,信函写作者和阅读者都是忙碌的商务人士,其目的是快速获取或者输出信息,这就导致这类商务信函在实际应用中具有功能明确、简洁清晰等特点。

外贸函电写得好,不仅能为公司赢得新客户,也有助于促进和发展交易双方之间的关系;而质量不过关、表意模糊不清的函电,则可能引发矛盾,造成客户流失和业务终止。要写好外贸函电,不仅要具备一定的语言基础和业务知识,还要熟悉商务函电的书写格式和行文要求。因此,学习和掌握商务电邮写作的基本知识是尤为重要的。

1.2 Questions 相关问题

本章要解决的问题如下:
问题1:商务电邮的组成部分包括什么?各部分有哪些操作建议?
问题2:商务电邮的格式和正文段落的写作建议是什么?
问题3:商务电邮的3C原则及操作建议有哪些呢?
问题4:商务电邮有什么细节性的操作建议吗?

1.3 Answer 你问我答

1.3.1 商务电邮的组成部分:"1 + 4"

规范的商务电邮,其组成部分是"1 + 4"。其中这个1,指的是邮件的主题(标题)——subject;其他4个部分是邮件的主体,包括称呼(salutation)、正文(body)、敬意结尾(complimentary close)和签名(signature),具体如图1.1所示。

1.主题

商务电邮的主题是不能省略的,主题要简短清晰,与邮件的核心内容契合。比如:你发送的是一封关于纺织品的询价函,对应的主题可以是Inquiry for Textiles;或者,你发送的是一封订单信,那么主题就是Order No.123。

2. 称呼

我们平时写私人邮件的时候也是有称呼的,那么商务电子邮件的称呼有哪些不同呢?答案是注重细节和严谨性。

To:	Smith@hotmail.com

主题 → | Subject: | Order No.123 |

称呼 → Dear Mr. Smith,

正文 →

结尾 → Yours truly,

签名 → Monica Wang

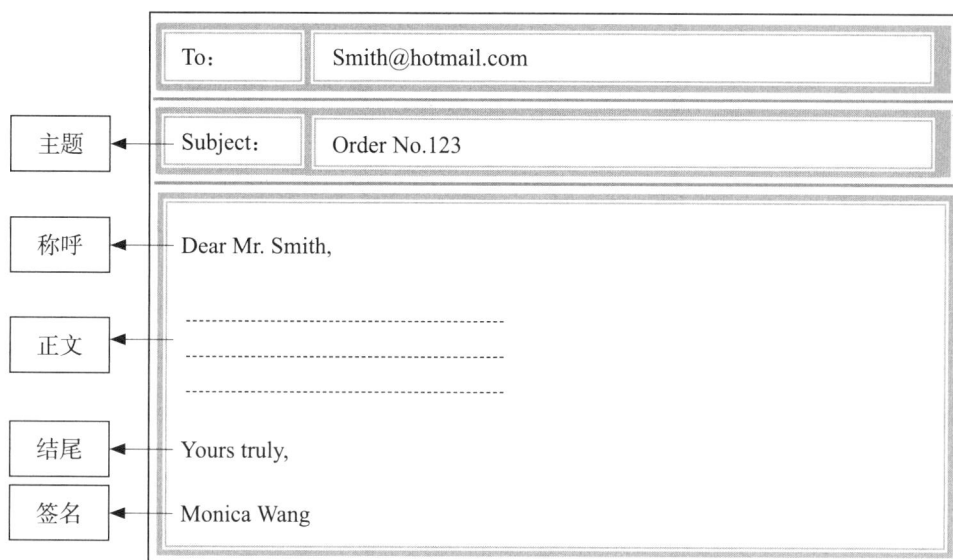

图1.1　商务电邮的组成

　　如果你第一次给潜在目标客户写商务邮件，只知道对方的一个邮箱，不知道打开你邮件的人是男是女，姓甚名谁，这个时候建议用Dear Sir。请记住细节：Dear中的D要大写，Sir中的S要大写，Sir后面加逗号。

　　如果已经知道客户姓名，建议用Dear Mr.×××/Dear Ms.×××。例如，客户是Jack Smith，Jack是他的first name（名），Smith是他的family name（姓）。我们可以用Dear Mr. Smith，随着业务的持续交往，我们可以直呼其名，如Dear Jack。

3. 正文

　　商务电邮正文撰写，建议篇幅为2~4段，每段1~3句，一事一段。这个是基于实战经验的建议，在之后各章的分项专题中将结合具体内容进行学习和讲解。

4. 结尾

　　商务电邮结尾部分有两种常用写法：一种是正式结尾，如Yours truly/Yours faithfully/Sincerely yours。要注意规范：两个单词可以互换先后位置，可以是Yours truly，也可以是Truly yours；首字母要大写，第二个词后面加逗号。

　　另一种是非正式结尾，表示亲密和熟悉，如Best regards，或者只写Regards，Rgds，都是可以的。

5. 签名

　　初次交往和提供报价等关键信息的沟通邮件，建议采用包含多种信息的签名群，以便对方迅速便捷地联络你，其内容包括姓名+职位+公司名+地址+电话+传真+公司网址等。在本教材中，我们称之为"全署名"。在其他的情况下，可以酌情用姓名+职务+公司，或仅仅用名字，参考范例如图1.2所示。

```
Monica Wang, Sales Manager
ABC Textiles I/E Co., Ltd.
Ningbo, China
Tel: 86-574-12345678
Fax:86-574-87654321
Website: www. abctextiles.com.cn
```

```
Monica Wang, Sales Manager
ABC Textiles I/E Co., Ltd.
```

```
Monica Wang
```

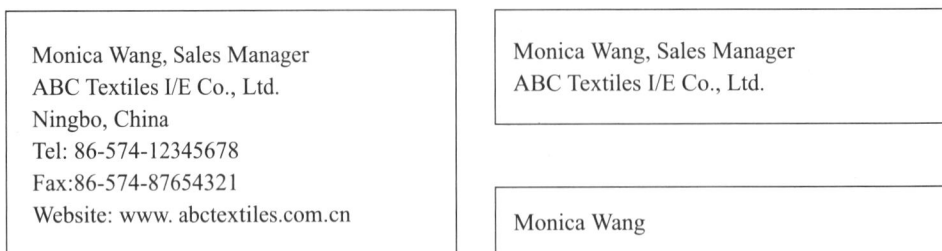

图1.2　签名参考范例

1.3.2 商务电邮的格式和3C原则

1. 商务电邮的格式

商务电邮的格式常用的有两种:齐头式和缩进式（见图1.3）。

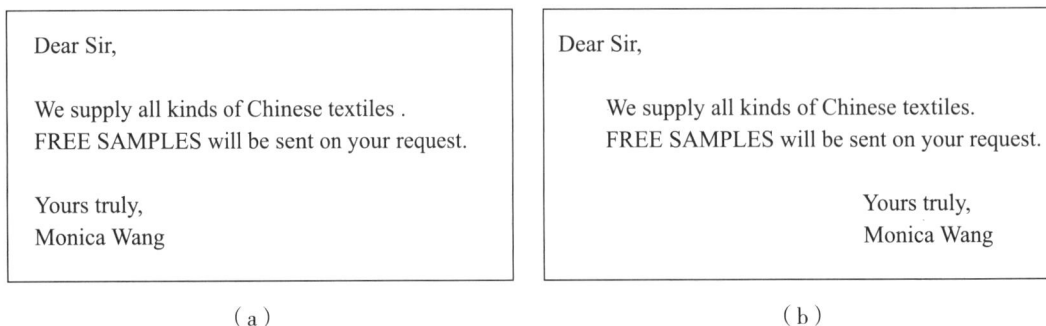

```
Dear Sir,

We supply all kinds of Chinese textiles .
FREE SAMPLES will be sent on your request.

Yours truly,
Monica Wang
```

```
Dear Sir,

    We supply all kinds of Chinese textiles.
    FREE SAMPLES will be sent on your request.

                            Yours truly,
                            Monica Wang
```

（a）　　　　　　　　　　　　　　　　　　　　（b）

图1.3　商务电邮格式

图1.3（a）是齐头式：邮件的每一行都从左边缘对齐写起,不同部分之间留有空行。这种格式看起来整洁清晰,阅读舒适且操作简单,是常用的格式。

图1.3（b）是缩进式：称呼顶格,正文每段的开始都缩进相同数格,结尾和签名中间偏右。

视频1.2

此外,还有一种混合式,即结合了齐头式和缩进式两种方式的特点,但这种格式较少采用。本书样函均采用齐头式格式,同时也建议学习者在撰写商务函电时首选齐头式。

2. 商务电邮的3C原则

写好商务函电,要遵循3个主要原则,即3C原则：conciseness（简洁）、clarity（清楚）、correctness（正确）。

第一个原则是简洁。商务人士每天需要处理大量的事务。我们可以换位思考一下：如果是你,邮箱里收到一封长篇大论的邮件,还是来自某个陌生人的,你是否有耐心仔细地读完这封邮件呢？答案一定是否定的。所以在撰写商务邮件的时候,要注意简洁,尤其在业务开发阶段或者双方初次沟通的时候,篇幅要尽可能短（short）,邮件要直切主题,长话短说,让内容简单易读。

第二个原则是清楚,即表意要明确,词句要清晰,避免使用容易引发对方歧义的双重意思或模糊表述。清楚和简洁相辅相成，摒弃传统函电中的无意义套话，可使双方的交流更加顺畅。

第三个原则是正确。商务函电具有特殊性，它的目的性和功能性都很强，函电中传递的信息必须是正确且准确的。除了正确的语法、标点和单词拼写外，还要注意专业词汇的精准、格式和细节的规范，以及数值的准确。

在一些外贸函电教材中，还提到了其他4个原则，包括concreteness（具体）、courtesy（礼貌）、consideration（体谅）、completeness（完整）。连同上面的3C原则，可合并为外贸函电写作的7C原则。这些原则可指导提升外贸函电的写作水平。

3. 关于3C的操作性建议

第一是篇幅控制。一般情况下，正文篇幅建议2~4段。段落内容要条理清晰，一事一段。第1段，开门见山，用1~2句话表明写信意图，体现商务信函的功能性特征；第2、3段写具体内容，如果内容不多，3句话以内，可集中于一段阐述，如果内容较多，可另分一段；接下来就是结尾段，1~2句话结尾即可。

第二是词句用法。避免使用长句和从句，多用短句和简单的单词；能用一句话，不用两句话；能用一个词，不用两个词。

第三是语法建议。多用被动句，少用主动句。

第四是写作习惯。养成写后通读、自我检查的习惯，常用换位思考来改进和提升。

1.3.3 商务电邮的其他操作细节

1. 邮件抄送问题：抄送栏不要忽略

首先，如果对方邮件发送过来，抄送栏是有其他人的，在回复时，要注意点击"全部回复"，以便对方公司的相关人员都能及时收到你的回复邮件。其次，如果你发送的邮件需要抄送本公司其他人，要记住在抄送栏内加上自己公司人员的邮箱，以便公司内部相关人员及时跟进你的邮件。

2. 签名问题：完整的署名，增加机会

关于邮件的签名部分，尤其是初次交往和提供报价等关键信息的沟通邮件，建议使用完整的署名，以便对方迅速便捷地联络你。完整的署名内容包括姓名+职位+公司名+地址+电话+传真+公司网址等。

视频1.3

3. 附件和图片问题

在发送邮件的时候，有时候需要随同发送一些电子附件和图片，如公司简介、产品目录、价格表等。如果随附电子附件的，建议在签名之后把附件的明细列出来。例如，你发了两个附件：一个是产品目录，一个是价格表。我们可以在签名后如图1.4所示这样写。

如果随同发送一些图片，如产品明细图、包装细节等。方法有两种：在正文中直接插入或者放入附件一并发送。不管是哪一种情况，都要注意以下几点：

（1）尽量用常规格式的图片文件，如jpg或pdf格式，不要用其他特殊格式，避免客户的电脑由于没安装相应软件而无法打开。

（2）图片不能过大，如果是手机或相机拍好的照片，不要直接插入，要把照片大小调整合适后再发送,避免客户因网速问题而不便打开。

（3）如果有多个图片放入附件中一并发送,要先统一做好处理,分门别类整理好再放入附件发送。

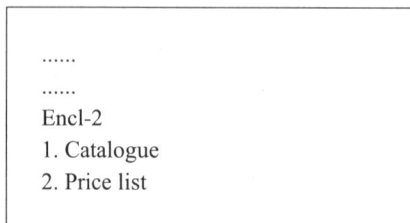

```
......
......
Encl-2
1. Catalogue
2. Price list
```

图1.4　附件明细

1.4　Summary 小结

商务电邮的内容结构被概括为"1＋4"。即主题、称呼、正文、结尾和签名。主题不可少,且必须与邮件正文的核心内容紧密契合;称呼可以是Dear Sir, Dear Mr. Smith, Dear Jack等;结尾可以是Yours truly, Regards等;签名可以是Monica Wang, Sales Manager/Monica这种形式,或者是包含姓名＋职位＋公司名＋地址＋电话＋传真＋公司网址等多种信息的全签名。

商务电邮的格式建议是齐头式:全部内容从左边顶格写起,各部分之间有空行;正文篇幅建议是2~4段,一事一段。

商务电邮写作的3C原则是简洁、清晰、正确。操作建议:多用被动,少用主动;多用短句和简单词汇;少用长句和复合句;写后要通读自查等。发送附件时,建议在签名后增加附件明细;随附图片:要用常规格式,图片不宜太大,多个图片要分门别类统一整理好再发。

1.5　Exercises 练习

I Multiple choice.

1. The complimentary close of a business email could be "_____".
A. Yours truly,　　　　　B. Faithfully yours,
C. Best regards,　　　　　D. Regards,
2. The three main principles of a business email are _____.
A. concise　　　B. clear　　　C. correct　　　D. comprehensive
3. The enclosures of a business email could include _____ etc.
A. sample　　　B. catalogue　　　C. price list　　　D. picture
4. Generally, the parts of a business email include _____.
A. subject　　　B. salutation　　　C. body
D. complimentary close　　　　　　E. signature

Key1.1

5. To John Smith , the following inappropriate salutations are " _____ ".

A. Dear Mr. John,　　　　B. dear John,　　　　C. Dear John,　　　　D. Dear Mr. Smith,

II Discussion.

What are the basic skills of a foreign trade salesman in your opinion?

1.6 Supplement & Extension 补充与拓展

商务书信的组成部分: "7＋6"

目前的外贸函电是以商务邮件为主要形式的,商务书信越来越少见了。但是作为外贸从业人员,对于规范化的商务书信格式,有必要了解一下。

商务书信的组成部分是"7＋6",就是7个标准部分加上6个可选部分,如图1.5所示。

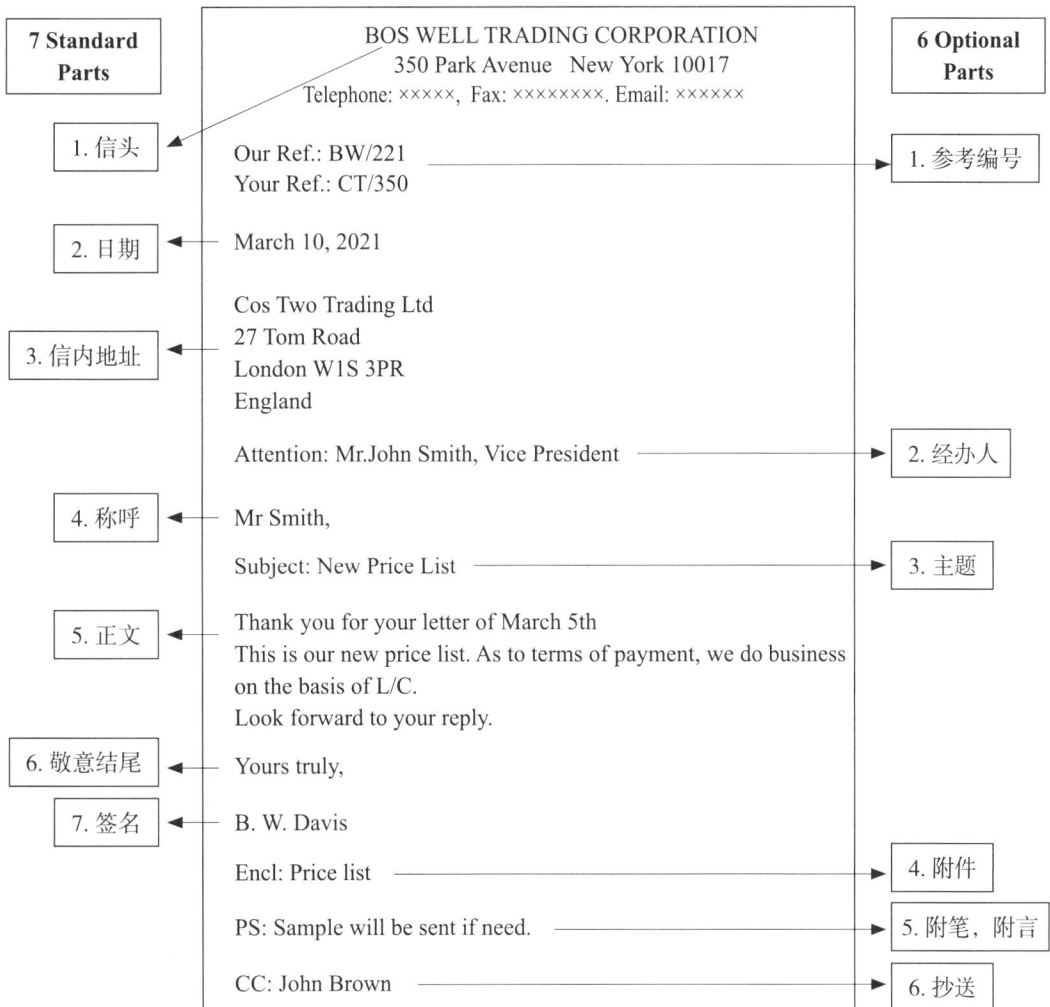

图1.5　商务书信的组成部分

7个标准部分是信头、日期、封内地址、称呼、正文、敬意结尾和签名。

第一是信头 (letter head)，包括公司名称、地址、电话、网址和传真等。信头通常位于信纸的最上端，位置居中。

第二是日期 (date)，位于信头下方，可以按照日—月—年，也可以按照月—日—年的顺序，年份用阿拉伯数字写出，月份建议用英文全称，日期可以是基数词，也可以是序数词，在年份前要加逗号。

第三是信内地址 (inside address)，指的是收信人的姓名和地址。这部分和信封上的内容是相同的，位置在日期的下方，每项内容单独成行，按照由小到大的顺序分项列出的。

接下来的4个部分和商务电邮是一致的，分别是称呼 (salutation)、正文 (body)、敬意结尾 (complimentary close)、签名 (signature)。

6个可选部分是参考号、经办人、主题、附件、附言和抄送。

第一部分是参考编号 (reference number)，通常在日期的上方。给信函编号是为了便于往来书信的存档和查阅。一般采用你方编号 (your ref.) 或者我方编号 (our ref.) 来进行信函编号。

第二部分是经办人 (attention line)，一般是在封内地址的下方，当发信人希望能将信函交给某个具体的人或部门时，可以加注这个部分。

第三部分是主题 (subject)，在称呼的下方。主题便于对方在阅读信函的正文前对信函的内容有所了解。

第四部分是附件 (enclosure)。假如信封内除了信纸外还有其他文件，可在这个部分说明附件份数和内容。

第五部分是附笔、附言 (P. S.)。在写完信后还需要附加一些内容时，可以在这里补述，位置一般在签名和附件的下方。在很多情况下，这个部分是为了引起对方的注意。

第六部分为抄送 (carbon copy)，也就是C. C.。发信人如果需要将此信抄送给有关单位，就可以在最后这个部分写上C. C.，后面跟上抄送单位的名称。

信封的写法

信封的左上角位置是寄件人地址，中央偏右位置是收信人地址。地址内容的顺序是从小到大：姓名—公司地址—城市—国名等，具体如图1.6所示。

图1.6　信封的写法

Chapter 2

Pre-business Contact

业务开发专题
——零起点，教你速成

学习目标

☆知识目标

✓了解寻找客户和获取商务信息的渠道及方法；

✓了解业务开发信的标题设计思路；

✓掌握业务开发信的内容结构；

✓掌握业务开发专题常用词句。

☆能力目标

✓能够结合业务开发阶段的不同场景撰写对应的开发信；

✓能够比较并讨论不同开发信的优缺点；

✓能够列举提高开发信回复率的解决措施；

✓能够依据3C原则分析、交流并改写开发信。

2.1 Introduction 知识介绍

2.1.1 商务知识

业务开发专题的学习内容包括寻找客户和撰写开发信两个部分。

寻找客户是外贸业务的第一步。无客户无交易,如果没有客户或潜在客户,接下来的商务沟通和交易谈判就无从开展。寻找客户的渠道和方法有很多,既有基于传统外贸模式下的一些常用方法,也有运用互联网思维重塑的新渠道。在本章的补充与拓展部分,将介绍寻找客户的一些方法与技巧,以及开发信的标题设计,而本章主体部分主要学习如何撰写开发信的正文内容。

开发信是交易磋商之前买卖双方进行联络和沟通的功能性函电,可以是卖方发给买方,也可以是买方发给卖方。在外贸业务实践中,买方发送的开发信多以询盘的形式呈现,这部分内容将在第3章讲述。本章主要关注卖方发送的,以建立业务关系为目的的联络信函。

开发信的功能是宣传公司产品和开发客户,卖方在获取潜在客户的联系方式后,将公司的产品、服务、优势等通过邮件发送给这些客户,希望建立合作关系,共同发展。潜在客户在收到邮件后,如有意向,则会回复做进一步的沟通和谈判,从而开始持续性的交易磋商,直至确立交易合同。

2.1.2 信函结构

开发信的正文内容结构一般包括4项:信息来源、写信意图、公司或产品介绍、其他信息。

(1)信息来源:简要告知对方你是如何得知对方公司情况的。

(2)写信意图:表达写信目的,例如,希望与对方建立直接的业务关系等。

(3)公司或产品介绍:介绍公司业务范围或简要推介可提供的产品。

(4)其他信息:介绍自己公司的优势和特色。

作为买卖双方的第一封沟通联络信,开发信的签名部分建议"全署名",内容包括姓名+职位+公司名+地址+网址+传真+电话等。之后的其他联络信可以适当简化。

2.2 Task and Project 任务和项目

Task 1: 撰写第一封业务开发信

☞ 写业务背景与任务

ABC公司是宁波一家主营各类纺织品出口的外贸公司,Monica Wang是公司的新员工,本周是她上班的第三周。在前两周,Monica已经对公司经营的各类产品进行了初步的认知和了解,从这周起Monica开始了她的业务开发第一步——浏览各类网站,搜索求购信息，寻找潜在客户。当她在网络上浏览的时候，注意到这样一条求购信息：

> We are in the market for textiles, pls contact: BBB@hotmail.com

Notes

1. be in the market for 想要购买或者欲采购
2. textiles 纺织品

　　ABC公司是经营各类纺织品的出口贸易公司，质量很好，价格也有优势，产品在国内外销路一直都不错。Monica很兴奋，她感觉商机来了，展示自己能力的机会到了。

☞ **写作任务**

　　请以ABC公司业务员的身份，依据上述背景撰写一封业务开发函电。相关要求如下。
（1）基本符合3C原则：正确、简洁、清晰；（2）段落建议：2~4段；（3）格式：齐头式。
　　这是Monica的第一封业务开发信，如果你就是Monica，该如何完成这个任务呢？

例2-1：第一封业务开发信

To: BBB@hotmail.com

Subject: Textiles Supplier—ABC Co.

Dear Sir,

Glad to learn from website that you are in the market for textiles. We would like to enter into business relations with you.

We supply all kinds of Chinese textiles with good quality and reasonable price. The latest e-catalogue is enclosed. Please let us know if you are interested in any of the items.

Look forward to your reply.

Yours faithfully,

Monica Wang

ABC Textiles I/E Co., Ltd. Ningbo, China

Tel: 86-574-12345678，Fax:86-574-87654321

Website: www. abctextiles.com

Encl: The Catalogue from ABC Textile

Notes

1. subject：主题（标题）

2. supplier：供应商

3. enter into business relations with：与……建立业务关系

4. good quality and reasonable price：质优价廉

5. e-catalogue：电子目录

6. enclose：随函附上，enclosure附件，可缩写为encl或Enc

7. item：商品或项目，常指目录或价格表中所列的货品

8. look forward to：盼望，期待

　　这是一封三段论商务邮件，首段采用省略主语写法，用两个句子说明了信息来源和写信意图。第二段是关于公司产品介绍和其他信息的，其中第1句和第3句看上去较长，但因为用词简单，理解起来难度不大。中间的第2句运用被动语态，使表意清晰，并具简洁性。结尾句也是采用省略主语的简洁写法。

　　这封样函的内容结构涵盖了业务开发信的4项基本内容，是常见的表达建交意愿和介绍公司产品情况、体现业务开发功能的商务邮件。全文呈纺锤形，框架清晰，词句运用体现了一定的专业性，适于初学者学习借鉴，并在此基础上进一步改进和提升。

Task 2：讨论与改写

☞ 讨论与分析任务

　　四人一组将例2-1的样函和自己撰写的业务开发信进行比较，分析各自的优缺点，并归纳从主题到内容方面，有哪些细节不同和可相互借鉴之处。

📹 视频2.2

☞ 改写任务

　　请在例2-1的样函的基础上进行改写，使得简洁清晰性更为突出，同时增加至少一个亮点或卖点（比如免费样品）来吸引对方，以提升客户的兴趣和回复率。

例2-2：提供免费样品的开发信

To: BBB@hotmail.com

Subject: Textiles Supplier—ABC Co.

Dear Sir,

Glad to hear that you are in the market for textiles. We supply all kinds of Chinese textiles with good quality and reasonable price.

The latest e-catalogue is enclosed. Pls do not hesitate to contact me for any questions. FREE SAMPLES will be sent on request for your evaluation.

Yours faithfully,

Monica Wang

ABC Textiles I/E Co., Ltd. Ningbo, China

Tel: 86-574-12345678，Fax:86-574-87654321

Website: www. abctextiles.com

Encl：The Catalogue from ABC Textile

Notes

1. contact me：与我联系

2. sample：样品、样本；free sample 免费样品

3. on request：根据要求，一经要求

4. for your evaluation：供你方评估/参考

　　这封信是例2-1的样函的改写函。首先依据3C中的简洁性原则进行了内容删减和改动：去掉了原文中非必要的第二句，并对个别表意进行了调整，全文由三段论变为两段论，使得表意更为简洁清晰。其次，在第二段用大写黑体字强调了可提供免费样品，以吸引客户关注。

☞ **思考与讨论**

　　问题1：改写后的开发信有哪些优点或不足？

　　问题2：信息来源是开发信必不可少的吗？

　　问题3：写信意图是开发信必不可少的吗？

　　问题4：提供免费样品是提高开发信回复率的唯一法宝吗？

　　问题5：如果开发信发出后没收到回复，还有什么其他方法？

2.3 Actual Case Letters 实战信函

　　业务开发信的目的是传递建交意愿，开发潜在客户。但在实际业务中，开发信发出后被客户回复的概率很小，利用开发信寻找客户往往是大海捞针。

　　那么，怎么才能提高业务开发信的回复率呢？什么样的开发信会唤起客户的需求，被

客户优先回复呢？如何才能写出引起客户兴趣的开发信呢？

以下开发信的原始素材都是外贸业务往来的实战邮件，结合教学目标做了适当修改。

例2-3：极简特色开发信

To: BBB@hotmail.com

Subject: Textiles Supplier—ABC Co.

Hi Sir,

ABC Textiles Co. here, export textiles with good quality and reasonable price.

Also we have our professional designers to meet any of your requirements.

Any questions, call me, let's talk details.

Regards,

Monica Wang

ABC Textiles I/E Co., Ltd. Ningbo, China

Tel: 86-574-12345678，Fax:86-574-87654321, M.P: × × × × × × × × × ×

Website: www. abctextiles.com

Notes

1. export：出口

2. professional designers：专业的设计团队/人员

3. meet any of your requirements：满足您的任何需求

这是结合Task 1的业务场景并基于一封实战案例稍作修改的极简特色开发信，全文共三段三句话，语言风格轻松随意，表意简洁流畅，通俗易懂。其中第二段体现了亮点和优势，签名部分除公司联络信息外，还特别留下了手机号码。

☞ 思考与讨论

问题1：初次联系的开发信中称呼和敬意结尾一定要规范严谨吗？

问题2：开发信中要留下个人手机号码吗？

例2-4：强调信息来源的开发信

To: BBB@hotmail.com

Subject: Textiles Supplier—ABC Co.

Dear Mr. Smith,

Your firm has been recommended to us by Morris Co., with whom we have done business for many years.

As I know, you have interest in purchasing textiles from China. We supply all kinds of textiles to global market.

Please contact me for any questions.

Yours truly,

Monica Wang

ABC Textiles I/E Co., Ltd. Ningbo, China

Tel: 86-574-12345678

Website: www. abctextiles.com

Notes

1. firm：公司或企业

2. recommend：介绍或推荐

3. Co.：company的缩写，公司

4. have done business for many years：有多年的业务关系

5. purchase：购买

6. global market：全球市场

撰写开发信时，要避免以自我为中心的长篇大论式的公司介绍，但同时也要注意彰显不同。如果潜在客户是经由双方共同认识的老客户引荐的，就需要在信息来源中加以明确，以增加客户信任感，从而提升回复率。

例2-5：罗列公司优势的开发信

To: BBB@hotmail.com

Subject: Textiles Supplier—ABC Co.

Dear Mr. Smith，

Glad to find your e-mail address from website. Our company deals in the export of textiles.

Our advantages are as follows:
1. Own a professional R & D team.
2. Experienced in doing business with big customers.
3. Stable delivery time.
4. Free samples could be provided.

Any further questions, please do not hesitate to inform me.

Truly yours,

Monica Wang
ABC Textiles I/E Co., Ltd. Ningbo, China
Tel: 86-574-12345678
Website: www. abctextiles.com

Notes
1. deal in：经营
2. professional R&D team：专业的研发团队
3. customer：客户
4. stable delivery time：稳定的交货期

　　如果公司具备有别于其他同类供货商的优势，则可以采用罗列优势条目的开发信设计思路，以吸引客户并获得及时回复。

例2-6: 陈述公司优势的开发信

To: BBB@hotmail.com
Subject: Textiles Supplier—ABC Co.
Dear Mr. Smith,

We get your name and E-mail address from Alibaba. com that you are in the market for textiles.

Ten years experience, CE certificated and at Ningbo port are how we keep superior quality and competitive offers for global valued customers.

Our main products are various kinds of high quality and nice designed textiles. Here is our e-catalogue. Please contact me if any item is attractive to you.

Yours faithfully,

Monica Wang

ABC Textiles I/E Co., Ltd. Ningbo, China

Tel: 86-574-12345678

Website: www. abctextiles.com

Encl: The Catalogue from ABC Textile

Notes

1. Alibaba.com: 阿里巴巴平台

2. CE certificated: CE 认证，加贴CE标志的商品表示其符合环保和消费者保护等一系列欧洲指令相关要求

3. offer: 报价

　　在开发信中要体现你的卖点，陈述有别于其他同类供货商的特色和优势，适当地推销自己，让对方觉得跟你合作能有所裨益，从而吸引客户关注，成功开发潜在客户。

例2-7：展会后的跟进开发信

To: BBB@hotmail.com

Subject: Toy Supplier—ABC Toy Co.

Dear Mr. Smith,

This is Monica from Ningbo ABC Toy Co., Ltd. Thank you for your visit at our booth A228 during the Canton Fair and glad to know your interest in our Teddy Bear series.

After the fair, I have collected the details about Teddy Bears supplied at present, which might be helpful for you. Enclosed is our new catalogue and a form of the details, please kindly check it.

Besides, we have experience to handle OEM orders. Should you have any questions, pls do not hesitate to contact me.

Yours faithfully,

Monica Wang

Ningbo ABC Toy I/E Co., Ltd.

Tel: 86-574-12345678, Fax: 86-574-87654321

Website: www. nbtoys.com

Encl-2

1. The new catalogue from ABC Toy Co.

2. Some details about Teddy Bear

Notes

1. Canton Fair：中国进出口商品交易会，简称"广交会"

2. series：系列

3. detail：细节，常用作复数形式

4. OEM：贴牌生产，代工生产

5. order：订单

　　参加展会是很多公司选择推广产品的一种很重要的方式。展会之后，要及时归纳整理展会上搜集到的客户信息并及时跟进客户。在信函中要简单给出相关信息，唤起客户的回忆，同时也让对方感觉到自己的效率。

例2-8：邀请客户见面的开发信

To: BBB@hotmail.com

Subject: Meet in Ningbo

Dear John Smith,

We are pleased to hear that you will come to Ningbo next week. I am not sure about your schedule. If possible, please visit our company at your convenience.

Could you please advise your flight No.? It is our pleasure to arrange the pick-up at the airport and drive you to the hotel.

Yours truly,

Monica Wang

ABC Textiles I/E Co., Ltd. Ningbo, China

Tel: 86-574-12345678

Website: www. abctextiles.com.cn

Notes

1. schedule：日程安排，时间表

2. at your convenience：在你方便的时候

3. pick-up at the airport：接机

业务开发是交易磋商的前序过程，即便在网络沟通为主流的环境下，适时邀请客户面谈，依然是业务开发的一个重要环节。

例2-9：向客户询问到付账号的信函

To: BBB@hotmail.com

Subject: Sample Photos

Dear John,

Samples were just completed. Please check the photos in attachment.

Which express company do you prefer? Please advise your account for freight collect. Thank you.

Best regards,

Monica

Notes

1. attachment：附件

2. express company：快递公司

3. account for freight collect：运费到付账号

外贸业务开发阶段，经常会遇到关于寄送样品的问题。这里所指的样品是产前样，就是供货商为客户提供的公司现有的产前样品。对于能够提供免费样品的开发信，往往能够受到买方重视。但是，寄送样品的快递费该如何处理呢？

一般而言，初次建立业务关系，需要双方共同配合。例如，卖方提供免费样品，承担样品费，买方承担快递费，这样对双方都是公平的。在这种业务背景下，就可以撰写请客户提供到付账号的信函。

例2-10：请客户支付样品费的信函

To: BBB@hotmail.com
Subject: Sample Charge
Dear John,

The new samples were finished strictly according to your request. But please pay for film charge USD 300 by your side.

After order placed, you could deduct this cost when balancing the payment. Enclosed please find our bank account file. Please advise your opinion.

Best regards,

Monica

Notes
1. according to your request：按照您的要求
2. film charge：制版费
3. cost：费用，成本
4. balancing the payment：支付货款

对于金额大或者有特殊要求的样品，需要供应方投入各种制版费和操作费等杂费，这个时候就难以做到免费提供样品了。此时可以采用"客户付样品费，我方支付寄送费"的方式。对于这种情况，首先要对客户实话实说，说明不能免费的原因，让对方理解并接受。同时，还可以提出样品费在对方下单后，可在货款中抵扣。

2.4 Summary小结

业务开发信是属于客户前期联络阶段的往来信函，其功能是传递建交意愿，谋求合作。对于很多外贸新手而言，用邮件开发客户是一种最常用、最节约成本的有效方式。在没有老客户和没有参加展会当面沟通的情况下，只能通过多写、多发业务开发信来寻找商机。

本章以外贸新手在业务开发阶段的视角，展示并分析了10封业务开发信，内容涵盖全面，整体以简洁清晰为特色，篇幅不长，适合初学者借鉴和参考。

开发信写作的注意事项如下。

2.4.1 标题要明确

标题是介绍信函主要内容的一个短语，开发信的标题尤为重要，应明确而具体，能够吸引客户关注。在本章的补充与拓展部分，将讲解如何设计开发信标题，以及解析经典标题。

2.4.2 邮件宜短不宜长

随着沟通方式的日趋便捷化，函电的篇幅总体趋向短小化，文风也更为多变。开发信作为双方初次沟通的信函，尤其应注意遵循简洁化原则。撰写开发信要避免长篇大论地介绍自己公司或工厂情况，或者为了炫耀英文水平，运用过多的长句和复杂句。应结合收信人的国别和具体情况，按照"2~4段、每段1~3句"的篇幅合理布局。具体业务中，如果客户是东南亚企业或中小型公司，建议函电尽量短小，突出重点，用词也应避免过于正式和生僻。如果客户是欧美的中大型企业，对企业文化和业务员素质较为重视，则往来函电一定要注意规范性和严谨性，用词不能过于口语化，以体现公司和个人的专业性。

2.4.3 关于群发和重复发送

发送开发信如大海捞针，需要极大的耐心和恒心。多数开发信在实际操作中都是群发或重复发送的，但在群发或重复发送时要注意八字操作要点：主题差别、适当修改。可以通过在邮件主题中加上客户公司的名称来淡化群发氛围，要做好记录，并结合发送时间和内容做适当修改，避免同样内容的邮件在不同时间发送给同一个客户。

2.5 Useful Words & Expressions 实用词汇及短语

1. market

n. 市场；需求；销路；交易；市价

Good ware makes quick markets. 好货销得快。

global market 全球市场

international market 国际市场

marker place 集市；市场

a market index 市价指数

come to the market 上市

find a market 找销路

good/poor market 畅销/滞销

be in the market for... 欲采购或想要购买……

We will contact you as soon as the new model comes to the market. 一旦新品上市，我们定将与你方联系。

We are trying to find a market for this article. 我们正在努力为此项商品找销路。

There is a poor market for these articles. 这些商品滞销。

One of our customers is in the market for Chinese green tea. 我方一位客户想要购买中国绿茶。

v. 销售；推销

We will try to market this product at our end. 我方将在我地设法推销该产品。

marketable

adj. 适销的；畅销的

marketable goods 畅销货

marketer

n. 专营某种商品的商人或商店

a big gasoline marketer 专营汽油的大商店

marketing

n. 买卖；营销

marketing cost 销售费用

2. supplier

n. 供应商，常指从图纸、制造到交货的供应商

a leading supplier of computers in the UK 英国一家主要电脑供应商

supply

n. & v. 供应

Supply now exceeds demand on our market. 现在我方市场供过于求。

We can supply all kinds of leather shoes. 我们可以供应各类皮鞋。

vendor *n.* 供货商/供应商；零售小贩（常指作为中间人的供应商或经销商）

retailer (or retail dealer) *n.* 零售商

wholesaler (or wholesale dealer) *n.* 批发商

3. enter into business relations with... 与……建立业务关系

相似的表述：establish/set up business relations with…

We would like to enter into direct business relations with you. 我们想和贵方建立直接的业务关系。

4. quality

n. 质量

Quality is the essence of this order. 质量是这笔订货的关键。

good quality and reasonable price 质优价廉

fair average quality (F. A. Q.) 大路货；良好平均品质

adj. 高质量的

This is a quality product. 这是一种高质量的产品。

5. catalogue

n. 商品目录（也可写作catalog）

e-catalogue 电子目录

latest catalogue 最新目录

illustrated catalogue 图文并茂的目录

catalogue for the standardized parts　标准化零件目录

classified catalogue 分类目录

pamphlet *n*. 小册子

leaflet *n*. 免费派发的活页宣传单

6. enclose

v. 随函附上

We enclose a copy of our price list. 我们随函附上我方价格表一份。

也可表意为：Enclosed please find a copy of our price list.

过去分词enclosed可用作名词，前面加定冠词。

We believe you will find the enclosed interesting. 我们相信贵方对附件会感兴趣。

enclosure

n. 附件；装入物（缩写为：Encl. or Enc.）

The envelope contains a check for USD 100 as an enclosure. 信封里有张100美元的支票。

相似的表述：attachment 附件，常用于电子邮件的附件。

7. item

n. 项目；条款；（商品的）品种

This is the best-selling item in this line. 这是这类商品中最畅销的品种。

We are also working on the other items and will call you as soon as possible. 其他项目也在进行中，将尽早电告。

8. let us know请告知

相似的表述：inform sb. of sth.

Please inform us of the market situation on your side. 请告知你方市场情况。

9. look forward to 期待

to 是介词，后接名词或动名词

Look forward to your reply. 盼回复。

We are looking forward to receiving your early reply. 期盼早日收到回复。

10. contact

n. & *vt*. 与……联系（接洽）；联系；交往

Please contact our local agent for further details. 详情请向我们当地代理商咨询。

We have been in contact with that firm for nearly three years. 我们与那家公司有近3年的交往。

11. sample

n. 样品

Quality must be up to sample. 质量必须完全与样品相同。

The business is not done on the basis of sample. 这笔生意不是根据样品成交的。

free sample 免费样品

counter sample 回样；对等样品

12. request

n. & v. 请求

As requested, we are sending you herewith our commercial invoice in duplicate. 按照要求，随函寄去商业发票一式两份。

We give you a list of our goods by your request. 我们按照你方要求提供一份货品清单。

on request 一经要求就……

Catalogues will be sent on request. 目录一经你方要求即可寄送。

13. for your evaluation 供你方评估

for your examination 供你方检验

for your reference 供你方参考

for your information 特告知你方

for your perusal 供详细审阅

14. export/import

n. & v. 出口/进口

We are interested in the import and export of foodstuffs. 我们对进出口食品有兴趣。

We used to import silicon sheets before, now we export them. 以前我们总是进口硅钢片，现在出口这项产品了。

exporter/importer 出口商/进口商

They are leading exporters of electric goods. 他们是电器用品主要出口商

复数：exports/imports 出口货/进口货

What are the chief exports of New Zealand？ 新西兰的主要出口货是什么？

export volume 出口量

15. purchase

v. & n. 购买；采购；购买项目或所购货物（常用 purchases）

We are purchasing these goods for our own account. 这些货是我们自己买的。

Regarding the balance of our purchases, please wait for our shipping instruction. 关于我们所购货的余数，请等我们的装运要求。

buy 和 purchase 都作动词"购买"解，buy 是一般用语，purchase 用于较正式或规模较大的采购和购买。

16. recommend

v. 推荐；建议

The seller recommends buying a small quantity for trial. 卖方建议购买少量试试。

We recommend that you contact them directly for your requirements. 我们建议你们直接

同他们联系沟通你方的需求。

17. Co.

company公司的缩写；company 不仅用于名称中也可泛指任何规模的公司。

Corp. 是corporation的缩写，一般指大公司，多用于名称中。

Inc. 是incorporated的缩写，指联合企业。

Line(s): *n.*(轮船、航空、航运等) 公司

Atlantic Container Liner 大西洋集装箱海运公司

office：*n.* 公司，多与head、home、branch等连用

3M China Limited Ningbo Branch Office 3M中国有限公司宁波分公司

18. competitive

adj. 有竞争力的

competitive price 竞争价格

competitive edge 竞争优势

competitive capacity 竞争能力

If your price is competitive，we will place an order with you. 如果贵方价格有竞争力，我们将发出订单。

Your products have no competitive capacity in our market. 贵方产品在我方市场上没有竞争力。

compete

vi. 竞争

We must compete with other suppliers in the price of the products. 我们必须在产品的价格方面与其他企业竞争。

competition

n. 竞争

Competition is getting keener in the cotton market. 棉花市场的竞争日趋激烈。

competitor

n. 竞争者

We trust our products can defeat the competitors. 我相信我们的产品可以打败竞争者。

19. specialize in 专营；经营

也可表达为：handle in，engage in，deal in

We specialize in the import and export of arts & crafts. 我公司专营工艺品进出口业务。

20. line

n. 行业；生意；航线；(商品的) 种类

best line 高级品

in this line 在这个领域；在这个行业

air-line 航线

We are going to present the full line of our leather products at Canton Fair in autumn this year. 我们将在今年的广州秋交会上展出各式各样的皮制品。

The company has been in this line of chemical industry for 10 years. 这个公司从事化工行业已经10年了。

in line/out of line with 相符合/与……不符合

Your price is entirely out of line with the market. 你方价格与市场价完全不符。

21. trade

n. & v. 贸易；行业；从事贸易；经营

In recent days, there has been a slow down in our trade with you. 最近我方和你方的贸易有所减少。

We do not trade with them. 我们不和他们做生意。

They trade mainly in cotton piece goods. 他们主要经营棉布业。

22. deal

n. & v. 生意；做生意；经营；处理；和……有关

We have come to a deal with an American customer. 我们已同一位美国客户达成了一单生意。

We have dealt with the Tom company for 10 years. 我们与汤姆公司做了10年的生意。

Deal with a man as he deals with you. 以其人之道还治其人之身。

The report deals with Hong Kong market. 该报告是有关香港市场的。

deal on credit 信用交易，赊账买卖

dealer

n. 商人；商号

a dealer in furs 毛皮商

23. manufacturer

n. 制造商；厂商

manufacture

v. & n. 制造；制造业（品）

manufactured goods 制成品

silk manufactures 丝织品

the textile manufacture 纺织业

We have passed on your samples to our manufacturer and expect to be able to send you our counter samples in a week. 你方来样已送交厂方，估计一周内能给你方寄去回样。

24. R & D 市场调研与开发

R & D全称为Research & Development，指公司内部负责市场调查和开发的专业机构或团队。

25. enjoy high reputation 享有盛誉

类似表述：enjoy a good market 畅销

26. OEM代工生产或贴牌生产

OEM是original equipment manufacturer 的缩写，原始设备生产商，亦为定牌生产或授权贴牌生产。指供应商按照客户的委托生产或代工生产，产品的要求、包装、设计等均由客户提供。

ODM: original equipment manufacturer，原始设计制造商。意为制造商有自己的设计团队，可以应客户要求对客户公司产品做修改或根据要求为其设计产品并生产。

OBM: original brand manufacturer，或 own brand & manufacturer，原始品牌制造商。指工厂经营自有品牌，或生产商自行创立产品品牌，生产、销售拥有自主品牌的产品，一般是规模企业，资金雄厚且拥有自己的研发设计队伍。

27. order

n. & v. 订单/订购

名词order常与动词make、send、place等连用，如果表示订购某项货物，后常接介词for。

We will place a large order with you next month. 下个月我们将向你方大量订货。

If your price is in line，we will send you an order for 6,000 sets. 如果贵方价格与市价相符，我方将订购6,000台。

If you allow us 10% discount, we will order 20,000 sets. 如果贵方给予10%的折扣，我们将订购2万台。

28. under separate cover 另行邮寄；另封

也可表述为by separate post/mail。

We are sending you catalogues under separate cover. 目录将另邮寄出。

29. charge

n. & v. 费用/收费

Samples will be sent free of charge. 免费寄送样品。

He is charged 5 dollars for mending a pair of shoes. 他修了一双鞋，被要了5美元。

30. payment

n. 支付，付款

Both sides have agreed on the payment terms. 双方就付款方式达成一致。

terms of payment 支付方式，付款方式

pay

v. 支付

How much do you pay for it? 你付了多少钱买那个东西？

It will pay to do that business. 做那桩生意是值得的。

payer *n.* 付款人

payee *n.* 收款人

2.6 Useful Sentences 实用语句

1. We have obtained your e-mail address from China Council for the promotion of International Trade in Beijing who had informed us that you are one of the leading importers of light industrial products in your country.

我们从北京的贸促会获得贵方邮件地址，并得知贵公司是贵国轻工业品的主要进口商之一。

2. Your firm has been kindly recommended to us by Messrs. J. Smith & Co., Inc., in New York, as large importers of furniture.

纽约史密斯有限公司向我们介绍，贵公司是家具业的主要进出商。

3. We owe your name and address to the Paris Chamber of Commerce, through whom we have learnt you are importers of table-cloth.

承蒙巴黎商会告知贵公司名称和地址，得知贵公司是桌布进口商。

4. We take the liberty to introduce ourselves as exporters of silk piece goods, which we have been exporting to Europe and Japan.

我们冒昧地向贵方介绍，我们经营丝绸商品，并常年出口欧洲和日本。

5. As the cameras you need happen to fall within the scope of our business, we hope to establish direct trade relations with your company.

贵方需要的照相机正好属于我们的业务范围，因此希望能与贵公司建立直接的业务关系。

6. Glad to hear that you are in the market for Chinese black tea, we have been in this line for many years.

很高兴得知贵公司想要购买中国红茶，我方已经营该类产品多年了。

7. We specialized in the export of Chinese arts and crafts.

本公司是专营中国工艺品出口的公司。

8. Pls visit our website to know more about our products: www.×××.

请浏览我们的网站了解更多的产品信息。

9. We supply handicrafts to Europe with good quality and competitive price.

我们的手工艺品出口欧洲，品质不错，价格有竞争力。

10. Art No. 23 BT is our recent development of this line of products with superb quality, fashionable design and competitive price.

第23BT号货物是我们最新开发的新品，这种新产品品质优良、设计时尚、价格具有竞争力。

11. We have been engaged in manufacturing electronic machinery of all specifications for over 20 years and exporting them to users all over the world, enjoying a good reputation.

我公司制造各种规格的电子机械产品已有20多年历史，并一直向世界各地的客户出口，且享有良好声誉。

12. Attached some photos for your view, for our hot-selling items.

附上一些图片供您参考，都是我们的热卖产品。

13. Enclosed please find our price list and brochure for our new products.

随函附上我公司新产品的价目表和商品小册子。

14. As to our credit standing, please refer to Bank of China, Ningbo branch.

关于我方资信情况，可向中行宁波分行咨询。

15. Since 2009，we have passed ISO9001, and all our products have CE certificate.

从2009年起，我公司已通过ISO9001，而且我们所有产品都有CE证书。

16. Our production capacity is 3,000 tons per month.

我们的生产能力是每月3,000吨。

17. We can offer OEM and design toys according to clients' requirements or samples.

我们可以提供定牌生产，并且可以根据客户的要求或样品设计玩具。

18. We supply power tools to EU market.

我们的电动玩具出口欧盟市场。

19. Nice and solid packing is our advantage.

漂亮且结实的包装是我们的优势。

20. If you have buying trip after this Canton Fair, please advise your time schedule.

如果您广交会后有采购行程，请通知我们您的具体计划。

2.7 Exercises 练习

I Translate the following words and expressions into English or Chinese.

1. 目录

2. 盼早复

3. 质优价廉

4. 国际市场

5. 另行邮寄

6. Canton Fair

7. OEM

8. enclose

9. R & D department

10. sample

II Choose the best answer.

1. We feel you may be interested in some of our other products and enclose a booklet _____.

A. to your reference   B. in your reference

C. on your reference   D. for your reference

2. Quotations and samples will be sent _____ receipt of your specific inquiries.

A. for   B. upon   C. with   D. to

3. We wish to introduce _____ the largest exporter of fabrics of high quality.

A. that we are   B. it that we are   C. ourselves as   D. ourselves to be

4. If the prices are _____ , we trust important business can materialize.

A. in line   B. in the line   C. on line   D. on the line

5. The quality of goods must be in strict accordance _____ the stated samples.

A. at   B. on   C. with   D. to

6. We are looking forward to _____ your further order.

A. receiving   B. receive

C. hearing from   D. being hearing from

7. We hope our latest computers will sell _____ in your market.

A. popular   B. a ready market   C. a fast seller   D. like hot cakes.

8. We specialized _____ all kinds of metals and are always ready to buy in large quantities.

A. in   B. from   C. on   D. at

9.We are please to _____ our latest price list for the goods you required.

A. close   B. enclose   C. in stock   D. put in

10. We are sending you _____ separate post the samples for the new season.

A. to   B. for   C. by   D. in

III Translate the following sentences into English or Chinese.

1. 我们可以根据您的要求提供免费样品。

2. 我们拥有专业的市场调研及开发部门。

3. 稳定的交货期是我们公司的重要优势之一。

4. 我们随函附上一份有插图的目录供贵方参考。

5. 如果有任何问题或意见,请发邮件或直接打我电话。

6. The items which you selected in our booth will be collected together in our showroom.

7. Our silk blouses have met with great overseas and always in great demand.

8. We are a trading company involved in import and export business throughout the world.

9. We are thinking of expanding business relations with India.

10. I would like to recommend you some new items which are suitable for US market.

IV Translate the following body of the letter into English.

这是我给您的第15封信。今天我想告诉您一些不同的东西,这是我在以前的信中没有提到的。

这些天,我研究了公司最近的业务数据,发现无论是加工工艺还是包装,都有很大的改进。我们在这个行业的优势越来越明显。我们的出色表现吸引了许多回头客。

我附上了我们的业务表和一些重要数据，以便您能更好地了解我们的公司。

如果您愿意给我们机会，我对我们的业务是非常有信心的。

希望这次您能给我们一个回复。

V Writing task.

Write a letter as per the business background and requirements.

宁波水木贸易公司（Ningbo Shuimu Trading Co., Ltd.）专营各类生活用品和礼品出口，如圆珠笔、充气产品、薰衣草袋、便携皂片等。同时也可根据客户的技术图纸或样品定制生产。

近日从阿里巴巴国际站了解到美国的一家公司（Green@Toytrading.com）在询购促销礼品。

请以公司业务员身份，遵循简洁、清晰、正确的3C原则，撰写一封业务开发邮件，表达希望与客户建立直接业务关系的意愿。

格式要求：齐头式。

VI Comprehensive practical training.

1. Read the following letter and discuss with your partners about its mistakes and shortcomings.

2. Rewrite the letter as per 3C principles.

Subject: Flashlight

Dear Purchasing Manager

Good morning my friend. Thanks for your time to read my Email. Glad to hear you are in the market of flashlight.

We are a manufacture of flashlight. Would you mind visiting our website: www.xxx. Wish our products will be helpful for your business.

Any questions, welcome here.

Yours faithfully,

Monica Wang

2.8 Supplement & Extension 补充与拓展

寻找客户的途径

没有客户就没有交易,开发阶段的首要任务是找到目标客户。搜集潜在客户的方法按照费用高低可归纳为三类。

第一类:需要资金投入较高的方法

1. 走向世界

具体包括在海外设立销售分公司、购并海外企业或直接在海外开展市场销售等。选择这种方法开发客户除了要有雄厚的资金外,还要有国际化的营销人才。这种方法的资金投入一般在人民币百万元以上。

2. 海外参展

一些国际性都市,如纽约、巴黎、汉堡、迪拜、莫斯科等,经常会有各种专业展会,可以通过联络各地贸促会或者外贸展会公司参展。一次参展的成本至少是5万元。

3. 国内参展

较为知名的是一年两度的春秋广交会,其一个摊位费最低也要3万元。其他综合性的外贸展会有上海的华交会、义乌的义博会等。另外,还有一些行业性的专业展会。这些展会的摊位费加上人员差旅费和其他准备工作费用,每次也在5万元以上。

4. 付费B2B网站

国内知名的付费网站就是阿里巴巴国际站。在此类网站上,买家可以免费发出采购信息,卖家则需要登记付费,少则几千元,多则数万元。

第二类:需要一定资金或成本的方法

1. 购买名单

海关数据、展会客商、行业信息等名单中有潜在客户信息,可以通过购买这些名单开展精准营销。

2. 网站推广

建立高质量的网站并通过搜索引擎优化SEO、点击广告、SNS营销等方式,导入潜在客户的流量与询盘。这种方式引来的潜在客户往往有较高的订购意向。

3. 加入国际协会:加入海外相关行业协会或其他组织。

4. 参与专业会议:这种方式非常高效,但是这种机会不容易得到。

5. 联系海内外政府机构和商业组织:如使领馆、商务部、贸促会、商会等。

6. 寻找代理商:可以通过寻找国内外的其他外贸公司或代理商开展业务和开发海外的渠道。

7. 客户推荐或朋友介绍

外贸人需要建立自己的商业人脉和信息分享网络,广交朋友,从而获得高质量的客户推荐或与别人分享订单。

第三类 免费的方法

1. 网络搜索

利用功能强大的搜索引擎，通过产品关键词不同的排列组合形式、产品图片、相关产品或者多语种、分国家等各种方法，充分利用网络这个免费工具搜寻目标客户。这是每个外贸人在业务开发阶段必走之路。

2. 专业参与

通过撰写博客或参与一些专业性的论坛，寻找与潜在客户沟通的机会。

3. 国际社交平台

如 facebook（脸书）、Twitter（推特）、LinkedIn（领英）等。

4. 直接自荐

直接联系来中国采购或者常驻中国的外商做自我推荐。

5. 免费网站

加入免费的B2B、B2C或C2C等网站。

开发信的标题（Subject）设计

外贸邮件的标题（主题）非常重要，尤其对于开发信而言，更是重中之重。一封陌生的外贸开发信被客户点开阅读的可能性不到1%，所以第一次撰写外贸开发信，最重要的因素就是标题。

一个设计得当、恰到好处的标题，会大大增加客户打开你邮件的机会，反之，一个不明确的模糊的标题，会让客户根本没兴趣去打开陌生人的邮件，你的正文内容写得再好，都是在做无用功。由于你的邮件标题写得不当，已经被你的潜在客户直接扫入了垃圾箱。

那么，如何写好标题，让你的邮件在众多的开发信中脱颖而出呢？这里有一些思路可供参考，请先看一组开发信的标题对比。

1. Subject：Establishing Business Relations

2. Subject：ABC Co. Seeking Cooperation

3. Subject：Textiles Supplier—ABC Co.

4. Subject：BBB Co./Textiles Supplier—ABC Co.

5. Subject：BBB Co./Wal-Mart Supplier-Textiles/ABC Co.

第一个标题"Establishing Business Relations"对应的中文意思是"建立业务关系"。这个标题明确了这封邮件的功能，让收件人从标题得知这是一封寻求建立业务关系的建交信，不是报价信，也不是订单函。

第二个标题"ABC Co. Seeking Cooperation"对应的中文意思是"ABC公司寻求合作"。在这个标题中出现了写信人的公司，这让收件人立刻知晓这是ABC公司发送的开发信。

第三个标题"Textiles Supplier—ABC Co."对应的中文意思是"纺织品供应商——ABC公司"。这是本章样函中使用的统一标题，是针对客户的需求设计的，同时也提到了自己的公司,应该说比第二个标题更具体了。

第四个标题是 "BBB Co./Textiles Supplier— ABC Co."。BBB Co., 是客户的公司名称,这个标题在第三个标题的基础上增加了客户公司名,表明这封邮件是专为对方公司撰写的,不是一个群发邮件。

第五个标题是 "BBB Co./Wal-Mart Supplier-Textiles/ABC Co."。其中的Wal-Mart是沃尔玛(全球最大零售商之一),标题传达的信息是:我们ABC公司是全球最大零售商沃尔玛的纺织品供应商。这个标题彰显了公司实力,在众多的开发信中容易脱颖而出。

通过这五个标题的对比,希望能够启发学习者的思路。在实际工作中,开发信的标题还有一些其他的设计。例如,用询问式语句来吸引收件人注意的提问式标题,或者通过优惠条款来抓住读者的承诺式标题,等等。

开发信标题实例与模仿

开发信的标题要能够激发客户的兴趣或者好奇心。在开发信标题的设计策略上,可以采用询问式、具体化表述、突出对方视角等方式和技巧。

请看这样一个标题: The Secret of Making People Like You(让别人喜欢你的秘密)。

这个标题是美国广告史上的一个经典文字广告标题,它是一个培训课程的宣传广告标题。这个标题成功地吸引了成千上万的读者去深入阅读,带动和影响了培训课程广告的正文信息。这个标题的设计,就很好地契合了我们上面提到的激发客户兴趣和突出对方视角这样的设计思路。

根据这个标题,我们来做外贸开发信标题模仿。例如,设计开发信的标题为The Secret of Making Your Boss Like You——Order from ABC Co.(让你老板欣赏你的秘密——从我们ABC公司订货)。

这个标题讲的是客户想知道的东西,是从对方的角度来诉说的,同时用了一种朋友间私下对话式的语气,而不是教科书式的说教。收到开发信的人也许会想:你们公司的产品就能让我的上司或老板赏识我、认可我吗? 我倒要看一下到底是怎样的东西。

在这种心理下,客户应该会有极大的概率点击开你的邮件,看一下你到底写了点什么。同时,在开发信正文中,要注意应该有吸引对方的卖点,比如具体说明:我们的质量、交货期等因素,而这些正是可以让客户的工作显得出色,在老板的面前凸显自己优秀的关键因素。

再来看一个标题: A Little Mistake that Cost a Farmer $3,000 a Year(一个让农民每年损失3,000美元的小失误)。

这也是美国广告史上的一个经典广告标题,这个广告当初是登载在一个以农民为主要受众的杂志上,也是一个以标题获得成功的案例。

这个标题的设计,利用的是"担心害怕损失"的心理。在很多情况下,"害怕损失"比"希望获利"对于客户来说更有吸引力。这个标题很容易让农民有兴趣去发掘:究竟是什么失误呢? 为什么说是小小的? 我有没有这样的小小失误? 别人每年因此损失了3,000美元,我会不会损失更多呢? 我得看看我有没有犯错。

结合这个标题，我们也来做一下外贸开发信的模仿。例如，这个开发信的标题是A Little Mistake that Cost a Import Company $5,000 a Year（一个让一家美国进口公司每年白白损失5,000美元的小失误）。

一般来说，人们在心理上，总是希望能够抵消、减少甚至完全避免任何损失的。以损失为突破口来设计开发信的标题，更容易吊住收信人的胃口。在接下来的开发信正文中，可以用讲故事的形式具体说明，什么情况或者哪些细节不注意或者掉以轻心，问题就会层出不穷。要尽量地把问题具体化，并将损失变为具体的金钱数值，来形象地说明对客户的影响。接着，再来说明我们非常注意这些因素，我们的做法都是以客户为核心的，也可以适当举例，更加鲜活地加以论述，同时也增加客户的代入感。

再举两个关于优惠商品诱惑的标题模仿的例子。

1. 标题模仿一

原广告标题是：Money-Saving Bargains from America's Diamond Discount House（来自美国钻石折扣商的省钱优惠商品）。

我们模仿的开发信标题是：Money-Saving Bargains from Chinese ABC Co.（来自中国ABC公司的省钱优惠商品）。

这个标题模仿运用的是价格优惠，但是冲击力还有一点不足。

2. 标题模仿二

原广告标题是：Save 20 Cents on Two Cans of Cranberry Sauce——Limited Offer（两罐酸果酱可省20美分——有限优惠）

我们模仿的开发信标题是：Save 20% on Your First Order——Cut Off Date ××××-××-××（你的第一笔订单可以有20%的折扣，优惠截止日期：某年某月某日）。

用具体的优惠折扣率和优惠截止期，可刺激和激发客户快速的反应。

在互联网营销时代，外贸开发信的撰写需要持续学习和不断研究。首先，搜集经典的广告标题，深入分析并借鉴模仿；其次，适当修正，变成自己的外贸开发信标题，逐步形成有针对性、有效果的外贸开发信标题库；最后，再结合标题撰写你的特色开发信正文，并在实践中提升。学习、思考、实践和持续改进，你的外贸开发信必将会为你带来丰硕的回报。

Chapter 3 Inquiries & Replies

询盘专题

——分类处理，区别对待

学习目标

☆知识目标

✓了解询盘的分类；

✓掌握不同种类询盘信的特点和相应的处理策略；

✓掌握询盘信和回复函的内容结构；

✓掌握询盘专题常用词句。

☆能力目标

✓能够运用所学知识并结合不同场景撰写询盘信及回复函；

✓能够依据3C原则比较并评析不同回复函的优缺点。

3.1 Introduction 知识介绍

3.1.1 商务知识

询盘专题学习内容包括了解询盘、回复一般询盘和回复具体询盘3个部分。

询盘(inquiry)是指交易一方准备购买或者出售某种商品,向对方询问买卖该商品的相关信息和交易条件。询盘是交易磋商4个环节(询盘、发盘、还盘、接受)中的第一环,是交易磋商的起点。在实际业务中,询盘多数是由买方发出,向卖方询问以价格为中心的各种交易条件,因此询盘又被称为询价。

询盘按照内容侧重,可分为一般询盘(general inquiry)和具体询盘(specific inquiry)两种。一般询盘是为了获取商品的一般性信息而发出的询盘,内容多为向对方索取商品目录、价格单、样品等。具体询盘是买方在有了比较明确的采购意向后就指定商品的交易条件进行询问,内容包括价格、包装、交货期、付款方式和折扣等,实际上就是请求对方报价或发盘。

在实际业务中,按照询盘信的来源,又可分为来自新客户和老客户两类。新客户询盘,可以是买方根据搜索到的信息,主动地向潜在的供应方发出邮件,询问相关产品的具体信息或索要资料,这也是买卖双方之间的第一封沟通联络信,兼顾建立关系和询盘双重功能。也可以是买方在收到来自卖方的业务开发信后,对其销售的产品有兴趣,回复其邮件询问产品的价格或索要资料。老客户的询盘通常是发给固定的业务员或者由公司指派专人处理,一般都是具体询盘。

回复函,又称回函或回盘,是对询盘信的回复,是对询盘方所需信息的回答。从法律上分析,询盘对买卖双方均无约束力,接受询盘的一方可给予答复,亦可不做回复。但在商业习惯上,收到询盘的一方应及时作出答复,以推进双方交易活动。

3.1.2 信函结构

询盘信的正文内容结构一般包括4项。

(1)介绍信息来源和己方公司情况。

(2)说明写信意图:明确想要购买的商品或货物。

(3)询问的内容:解释或罗列需要对方提供的信息或资料等。

(4)其他:强调关注点或表示订购的可能性等。

询盘信应尽量简短而具体,把相关要求和需要了解的信息阐述清楚。不同种类的询盘信,写作内容略有差异。

回复函的正文内容结构一般包括3项。

(1)表示感谢,建议提到来信日期或来信主题。

(2)逐一回复来信要求,如有不能满足的,需要有技巧地回复。

（3）告知其他信息。这部分的目的是吸引客户以便持续跟进，该部分要注意具体分析和差异处理。

撰写回复函时要紧密结合客户询盘的内容，具体问题具体分析解决，同时也要注意得体和周到。要善于激发对方的购买意愿，促进进一步沟通的行动，最终促成交易。

3.2 Task and Project 任务和项目

Task 1：认识和了解询盘

☞ *业务背景与任务*

ABC公司进出口部收到以下两封询盘信。（注：从此章开始，信函示例以标题和正文为主，其他部分适当略去。）

例3-1：询盘信1

Subject：Inquiry for Parts and Components of Automobiles

Dear Sir,

Your advertisement in *The Times* attracted us, and we are, at present, interested in your parts and components of various automobiles.

We shall be obliged if you will send us a copy of your latest catalogue and price list for our reference.

If the quality of your products may satisfied with us and your price may compare favorably with those of other supplies, we will surely have a long cooperation with you.

Yours truly,

John Smith

例3-2：询盘信2

Subject：Inquiry for LR Sofa

Dear Monica，

Have read your email of March 3.

We are interested in your LR Sofa，for 5 or 10 plus shipping to Sydney, Australia.

Could you provide your cost plus shipping expenses so that I may compare?

Regards,

Mike

Notes

1. inquiry：询盘，也可写为enquiry
2. parts and components：零部件
3. automobiles：汽车
4. advertisement：广告
5. *The Times*：《泰晤士报》
6. price list：价格单
7. for our reference：供我们参考
8. cost：成本
9. shipping expense：运费

☞ 讨论与分析任务

　　请两人一组讨论并分析：哪一个是一般询盘？哪一个是具体询盘？并概述原因。

Task 2：撰写回复函1：回复来自新客户的一般询盘

☞ 写作任务

视频3.2

　　请以ABC公司业务员的身份，参考本章商务知识中关于回复函的内容结构建议，结合下述要求，撰写对询盘信1的回复函。

　　要求1：请按照以下3个步骤完成写作任务，即分类—分析—回复。

　　第一步是分类：已经完成，该询盘信为来自新客户的一般询盘。

　　第二步是分析：请两人一组逐一思考并回答下列问题。

　　（1）此询盘需要优先处理吗？

（2）客户是贸易新手吗？

（3）客户的询盘要求，确定都能满足吗？是否需要与主管或同事沟通？

（4）还有什么其他信息可以提供吗？

第三步是回复：请各自独立完成该回复函。

　　要求2：部门主管说对于这种不明确具体情况的新客户，回函可随附电子目录，但是价格表目前暂时不要给，同时可以适当提下公司备有一些图片和样品可随时提供，以吸引买方的关注和后续的回复。

例 3-3：回复函 1

<u>Subject：Reply to Inquiry for Textiles</u>

Dear Mike，

Thank you for your inquiry of March 5 on textiles.

As requested, our catalogue is enclosed. Pls let me know if you are interested in some of the items. Our new price list is being prepared and will be sent to you soon.

Some pictures and samples will be sent on request.

Regards,

Monica Wang

ABC Co., Ningbo, China

http://www.××××××.cn

Tel：××××-×××××××, Fax：××××-×××××××

Notes

1. as requested：按照要求

2. pls: please的简洁写法

    这是一封三段论信函，一共五句话，是中间大两头小的纺锤形结构的询盘回复函。

    第一段用一句话对客户的询盘表示感谢，并提到了询盘信的日期和主题，简洁又清晰。

    第二段是主体段落，共三句话，针对询盘信的要求进行了回复，前两句满足客户要求，第三句是技巧处理。

    首先用了一个短语 "as requested" 作为开篇语，这个短语运用得体，隐含尊敬，让收件人读起来感觉愉悦，然后是逐一回复对方的要求。"Our catalogue is enclosed." 这里用的是被动语态而不是主动，显示了写信人的细节和专业。这一段的第一句和第二句，合起来构成一个完整的递进式意思表示，对应的译文是："按照要求，我们附上了目录。如果您对目录中的一些产品有兴趣，请告知。"这两句话既满足了对方索要目录的要求，同时也是我们的跟进性表意。第二段的第三句是一个技巧处理。这是一封对于新客户一般询盘的回复函，在原询盘中，客户还要求寄送价格表。如果我们由于某种原因，暂时不能或者不想发送价格表，这个时候直接拒绝是不可取的。这个回答提供了一种得体的暂缓处理方案。第三段是其他信息，只有一句话，简单但具有吸引力。这句话写得也很有技巧，隐含的意思是：我们是可以提供样品和照片的，但是需要您回复我们这个邮件，在提出具体需求后才会给。

这样能够促使客户回复我们这个邮件，只要建立了相互联系，生意就有希望。

这个询盘回复信，还有一个亮点在签名处。因为这是卖方发送的第一封信，所以卖方使用的是全署名，内容包括：签名＋公司名＋公司的网址＋电话＋传真号等。一方面体现了专业性和重视度；另一方面，客户如果对我们的产品有兴趣，也可能会打开我们的网站看一下。

这封回复函来自实战案例，是卖方针对新客户一般询盘的回复信。内容结构清晰，表意简洁，细节处理得体，适合参考借鉴。

Task 3：讨论与分析

请两人一组将例3-3的回复样函和各自撰写的回复函进行比较，对比分析各自优缺点。

Task 4：撰写回复函2：回复来自新客户的具体询盘

☞ **业务背景与任务**

结合例3-2的询盘信2的相关业务信息，整理如下。

（1）LR沙发，公司目前有两种材质：全皮（full leather）和织物（fabric），价格不同。

（2）向运输公司了解到：从产地到悉尼的海运费是USD35/cubic meter，一立方可装载LR沙发数量为2件，运输时间大约20天。

（3）该产品的生产周期一般是20天。

☞ **写作任务**

首先请重新阅读例3-2的询盘信，思考下列问题。

（1）此询盘需要优先处理吗？

（2）客户的询盘要求能够全部被满足吗？

（3）客户采购的数量和品类，还有增加的空间吗？

（4）回复时还有哪些信息可以附带告知吗？

（5）从询盘中，还能挖掘出其他潜在的信息吗？

然后请结合上述问题和相关业务背景，独立撰写针对询盘信2的回复函。

例3-4：回复函2

Subject: Reply to Inquiry for LR Sofa

Dear Mike,

Thank you for your inquiry of March 16.

Regarding the LR sofa. If you require with full leather this item cost, ×× USD/pc. If in fabric this item cost, YY USD/pc. I checked the shipping to Sydney about 35 USD/cubic meter and about 2 sets of LR sofa a cubic meter.

To produce them will spend about 20 days . To send them until arrival in Sydney about 20 days.

Kindly contact me for any questions. Pls visit our website to know more about our products: www.xxx.

Thanks and regards,

Monica

Notes

1. regarding：关于
2. full leather：全皮（材质）
3. fabric：织物（材质）
4. Sydney：悉尼（澳大利亚）
5. cubic meter：立方米

这封回复函也是来自实战案例，是卖方撰写的针对新客户具体询盘的回复信。正文共四段，与例3-3的回复函对比，内容篇幅有所增加，写作难度也有提升。

第一段用一句话对客户的询盘表示感谢。

第二段是结合客户询盘信的内容，用四句话逐一回复了客户的询价和运费情况。前三句是针对客户的询价，按照不同材质做了对应报价。最后一句是个长句，回复客户关于运费的询问。这句话体现了合理性和周到性：我们提供的是运费单价，同时告知客户每个立方货品的装载量，以方便客户结合采购数量自行核算总运费。

第三段两句话，这个部分不是针对客户询问进行的回复，而是其他信息。这里明确地告知客户我方的备货期和预计运输航程期，体现了专业性和周到。

第四段是结尾段，共两句。这一段采用适度引导，希望客户除了沙发外还能采购些其他产品，但是推荐的痕迹并不重，仅是一句带过，不易引起对方的反感。

在实际业务中，这种有针对性的具体询盘，被视为高质量询盘，要格外重视。应在第一时间给予回复，但是也不能在一收到询盘后，不做任何研究就贸然回复。效率很重要，时机也很重要。同时，撰写回复函时要紧密结合客户询盘的内容，因时制宜，具体问题具体分析解决。

3.3 Actual Case Letters 实战信函

在实际业务中，由于双方贸易关系及买方的关注点、英文水平等方面的不同和差异性，询盘信的内容也会有所不同。但是,无论是哪种询盘信,其内容都是以询问交易条件,要求提供相关商品资料为核心的。而卖方在回复询盘的时候,要仔细阅读询盘内容,按照客户询盘信中的问题或者咨询的内容逐一作答。

以下几篇询盘信及回复函,均来自外贸业务实践,结合教学目标和商业保密原则略做调整和修改,以供学习者学习和参考。

例3-5:一般询盘

Subject: Inquiry for Sports Wear
Dear Sir,

We obtain your name and e-mail address from the Bank of U.S. Commerce, New York and are interested in your Sports Wear.

We are now in the market for large quantities of Men's and Women's Sports Wear and would appreciate your sending us catalogues and price lists. In order to acquaint us with the material and workmanship of your products, we shall be grateful if you will send us relative samples.

Please give us detailed information on discount and terms of payment.

We hope this will be a good start for a long and profitable business relations.

Yours truly,

John Smith

Notes

1. obtain...from...:从……获悉/得知
2. Bank of U.S. Commerce:美国商业银行
3. sports wear:运动服饰
4. large quantities of:大量的
5. acquaint:使熟悉,使了解
6. workmanship:工艺,手工
7. discount:折扣
8. terms of payment:付款方式
9. profitable:有利的

这封信函是买方从第三方(一家银行)处得到卖方信息后,撰写的一封询盘信。全文

共四段，篇幅适中，从内容分析，可归为一般询盘。买方在询盘信中索要目录、价格表和样品，同时询问关于折扣和支付方式等交易条件。特别之处在于：买方在索要样品时，做了简要解释。整篇文字表意较为严谨。

例3-6：回复一般询盘

Subject：Reply to the Inquiry for Sports Wear

Dear Mr. Smith,

Thank you for your inquiry of July 6 for our Sports Wear.

As requested, we are enclosing some copies of illustrated catalogues and a price list. As for samples you asked, we will provide one suit each respectively for Men's and Women's Sports Wear after you choose the type you like. We trust that when you see them you will agree that our products appeal to the most selective buyer.

We allow a proper discount according to the quantity ordered. As to the terms of payment, we usually require L/C payable by sight draft.

We look forward to your early reply.

Truly yours,

Monica Wang

Notes

1. as for：关于

2. appeal to the most selective buyer：吸引最挑剔的买主

3. discount：折扣

4. quantity：数量

5. L/C：信用证

6. sight draft：即期汇票

7. L/C payable by sight draft：即期信用证

这封信函是卖方在收到例3-5的询盘信后，撰写的回复函，全文也是四段，篇幅适中。一般情况，回复函应同收到的询盘信段落数一致，或稍多于询盘信的篇幅，比如增加一段关于其他信息的说明或跟进促销等，这样会让对方感觉受到重视。同时，回复函的文风也要同询盘信保持一致，要避免对方的询盘信格式规范且表意严谨，而回复函却规范性不足或用词随意这类情况。

针对买方在询盘信中提出的相关要求和问题,卖方在回复函中采用分开处理,从而显得条理清晰。其中关于样品问题,首先表示可提供男士和女士各一套,但是需要在客户选择具体型号后才能寄送,然后又跟进表示己方产品质量优异,能够最大程度满足客户需求。一气呵成的连贯性表意,用词严谨,处理得当。

例3-7:具体询盘

Subject: Inquiry for Teddy Bears

Dear Monica,

We are glad to learn some details about your toys from your e-mail of June 7 and the attached catalogue.

We have studied your catalogue and are interested in your Good Boy Brand Teddy Bears. Please let us know your latest CIF Boston prices for different sizes together with your minimum order quantity and terms of payment, stating whether you would be able to effect delivery within 30 days after receiving our order.

Should your price be found competitive and delivery date acceptable, we intend to place a large order with you.

Your early reply will be highly appreciated.

Best regards,

John

Notes

1. brand:品牌
2. Teddy Bear:泰迪熊
3. CIF Boston:波士顿到岸价
4. minimum order quantity 起订量/最小订购量,缩写为 MOQ
5. effect delivery:交货
6. delivery date:交货日期

这封询盘信是买方在收到卖方的开发信后,给卖方的回复函,并在信中对具体产品提出报价等相关要求。这是一封具体询盘信,全文四段,篇幅适中。询盘信内容涉及具体的交易细节，如CIF价和MOQ等，并对交货期特别关注。该信函文风严谨且针对性强，容易引起卖方高度重视。

例3-8：回复具体询盘

Subject：Reply to the Inquiry for Good Boy Brand Teddy Bears

Dear John，

Thank you for your inquiry of June 10 for our Good Boy Teddy Bears.

As requested, we are sending you our latest price list for all sizes of subject goods for your reference. The MOQ for each size is 100 pcs.

As to the terms of payment, it is our custom to trade on the basis of an irrevocable L/C at sight, other details as per the price list.

We hope you will find our prices reasonable and look forward to your order.

Best regards，

Monica

Notes

1. pcs：pieces的缩写，数量词，意为只、件、条等

2. custom：习惯，惯例

3. irrevocable L/C at sight：不可撤销的即期信用证

4. as per：根据，按照

　　这封信函是卖方在收到例3-7中的具体询盘信后，撰写的回复函，全文也是四段，篇幅适中。针对买方在询盘信中提出的相关要求和问题，卖方一方面在回函中做了部分解答，另一方面随函寄送了详尽的价格表。从与买方的询盘信篇幅对比来看，这封回复函内容相对较少。

　　在实际业务中，对询盘信中的报价和交易要求，既可以在回复函中分别罗列出价格条款和其他交易细节来逐一回复，也可以采用随函寄送价格表或报价单等形式。但是，无论采用哪种形式，对于这类有针对性的具体询盘，都要尽量在第一时间准确而详尽地回复，从而给客户留下一个良好的印象。

例3-9：回复客户多种问题的询盘

Subject：Reply to Inquiry from YJY Co.

Dear Mr. Smith,

Thank you for your inquiry.

According to your questions, please find our reply as follows.

1. Are you a manufacturer?

——No, we are a trading company.

2. How many staff in your company?

——Roughly 55 in the office.

3. What is your main market? Turnover?

——Our main market is USA and Europe, and turnover is roughly 4 million USD per year.

4. Have you cooperated with any customers in New Zealand?

——Yes, we got orders from YJR and HKK in New Zealand.

5. Do you have interest to do our design items?

——Yes, we have big interest.

6. Is it possible to do O/A 45 days?

——According to our company rules, we could only do T/T or L/C at sight.

Please find our company profile in attachment. If you have any further questions, please let me know.

Best regards,

Monica Wang

Notes

1. staff：员工

2. roughly：大约

3. turnover：营业额

4. O/A：赊销

5. T/T：电汇

有些时候，客户的询盘信中有一大堆的问题，尤其是新客户，而回答这些问题就是一

个双方初次磨合的过程。因为客户对供应商完全没有了解，希望知道关于产品和公司的更多信息，这就需要在回复函中尽可能完整且详细地提供信息。这类信函如果回复及时，处理得当，往往会取得较好的后续效果。

例 3-10：向客户推荐新品的询盘

Subject：New Model Portable Hair Dryer

Dear John,

How are you recently?

Any news for the samples we sent you several month ago? Do you have some buying plans this year?

I would like to recommend you our new hair dryer model as below. Enclosed please find some photos for your selection.

Model: portable hair dryer
Item No.: SMH-0203
Power: 1900W
Function: 3 speed/3 heat setting
Color: all
Packing: color box

We have passed the testing and got the PSE certificate. Would you like to try a small order to test the market?

Regards,

Monica

Notes
1. portable hair dryer: 便携式电吹风
2. model: 型号
3. power: 功率
4. function: 功能
5. packing: 包装
6. PSE certificate: PSE认证是日本强制性安全认证，用以证明电机电子产品已通过日本《电

气产品安全法》或国际ICE标准的安全标准测试

不管是老客户还是新客户,都要经常保持互动,适当的跟进是必要的。但是,也要避免没有新意的打扰,推荐新品是一个很好的切入点。

3.4 Summary 小结

通过前期艰难的业务开发,终于有客户发来询问价格和产品详情的邮件,这就是询盘。从法律上分析,询盘对买卖双方均无约束力,接受询盘的一方可给予答复,亦可不做回复。但在商业习惯上,收到询盘的一方应及时作出答复,以推进双方交易活动。

本章以外贸业务流程为引导,侧重对于不同询盘处理手段的梳理和撰写对应的回复函,展示并分析了共计10封询盘和回复函。所选信函均来源于实际业务,内容涵盖全面,体现3C原则,便于学习者拓展思路,掌握询盘信和回复函。

询盘信和回复函写作的注意事项如下。

1. 询盘的形式

询盘可采用口头或书面的形式,如电话、传真、聊天工具和电子邮件等多种形式。

2. 询盘的内容

在撰写和发送询盘信时,买方应认真考虑向哪些地区发出询盘,以及在同一地区要与多少家供货商进行联系。询盘内容繁简均可,但应注意层次和效率,避免无效的往返磋商,浪费时间。

3. 询盘的效力和应用

询盘不具备法律上的约束力,只是探寻买或卖的可能性,询盘人可同时向若干个交易对象发出询盘。询盘不是每笔交易必需的程序,买卖双方可以越过该环节,直接沟通发盘或下单。

4. 询盘回复的原则:及时性和真实性

回复询盘的首要原则是及时:如因某种情况,暂时不能回复,建议先发一封信函说明原因,同时明确可回复的具体时间。其次就是真实性:要避免自作聪明地虚报价格或是夸大产品质量。

5. 询盘回复函的处理:分类处理,表意有别

建议按照三步处理:先分类,后分析,再回复。

(1) 对于来自新客户的一般询盘,建议围绕四问四答做针对性分析。这四个问题是:第一,此询盘需要优先处理吗? 第二,客户是贸易新手吗? 第三,客户的要求都能被满足吗? 第四,还有什么其他信息可提供吗?

(2) 对于来自新客户的具体询盘,建议围绕五问五答做针对性分析。这五个问题是:第一,此询盘需要优先处理吗? 第二,客户的要求都能被满足吗? 第三,客户采购的数量

和品类还有增加的空间么？第四，还有什么其他信息可附带告知么？第五，从询盘中还能得到其他信息吗？

在对客户进行深入分析的基础上，也要兼顾对行业和市场的把握，综合分析后撰写回复函。

3.5 Useful Words & Expressions 实用词汇及短语

1. inquiry

n. 询盘；询价；询问（也可写作enquiry）

general inquiry　一般询盘

specific inquiry　具体询盘

make/send inquiries　询问，调查

enquiry form 询价表

Thank you for your enquiry for carpets. 感谢你们对地毯的询盘。

We will make inquiries about the business possibilities of this new product of yours. 我们将调查一下你方这种新产品的销售可能性。

enquire

v. 询问；询价；咨询（也可写作inquire）

enquire about 询问……情况

enquire for 询购

They sent us an email to enquire about the market condition at our end. 他们发送邮件询问我方市场状况。

We acknowledge receipt of your letter of July 6 enquiring for alarm clocks. 你方7月6日询购闹钟的来信收到。

2. price

n. 价格；*v.* 开价；定价

price list 价格表，价目单

actual price 实际价格

unit price 单价

market price 市价

retail price 零售价

wholesale price 批发价

target price 目标价

cost price　成本价

selling price　售价

Business is possible if you raise the price by 3%. 如果你方出价能提高3%，可能成交。

The goods are priced too high. 此货定价太高。

The new product of ours is moderately priced. 我们这项新产品的定价适度。

3. cost

n. 成本

product cost 产品成本

production cost 生产成本

cost control 成本控制

transaction cost 交易成本

4. as requested 按照要求；应贵方要求

As requested, we enclosed our catalogue and price list. 应贵方要求，我方随函附寄目录和价格单。

5. regarding

prep. 关于，有关

Regarding the payment terms, let's decide next time. 有关付款方式，咱们下次确定。

Regarding the balance, we will advise you of the position in a few days. 关于余额情况，我方将于近日内告知贵方。

6. obtain… from… 从……获悉/得知

We obtain your name and e-mail address from Alibaba.com. 我们从阿里巴巴网得知贵方的信息。

建交函中表明信息来源的常用表达，类似的有：

We owe your name and address to…

Through the courtesy of…, we come to know your name and address…

7. acquaint

v. 使熟悉；使了解

to acquaint sb. with sth./be acquainted with 使某人了解某事

In order to acquaint you with our new products, we enclose here with our latest catalogue. 为使你方了解我们的新产品，现附上最新商品目录。

We are well acquainted ourselves with the market conditions in South America. 我们非常了解南美洲的市场行情。

8. workmanship

n. 工艺；手工

9. discount

n. & v. 折扣；贴现；减价；打折扣

The highest discount we can allow on this article is 10%. 我们对这项商品最多只能打9折。

Bills can be easily discounted in London. 汇票在伦敦贴现毫无困难。

If you can discount your price by 20%, we are ready to take 500 bales. 如果贵方价格能予以8折处理，我方将接受500包。

10. terms of payment 付款方式/支付条件

也可以写作 payment terms

11. profitable

adj. 有利的; 有益的; 可获利的

profitable fields of investment 有利的投资场所

profit

n. (常用复数) 利润

net profits 净利润, 纯利润

total profits 总利润

profit ratio (rate) 利润率

gross profits 总利润, 毛利

sell sth. at a profit 出售某物而获利

12. appeal

v. 对……有吸引力, 有感染力; 投其所好

We think the superb workmanship as well as the novel design will appeal to your customer. 我们认为其新颖的设计及高超的工艺会吸引贵方的顾客。

We trust you will find that its design and color will appeal very much to your market. 我们相信其设计及色彩定会受到贵方市场的热烈欢迎。

13. quantity

n. 数量; 大量; 多批 (用复数)

maximum/minimum quantity 最大/最小数量

average quantity 平均数量

estimated quantity 估计数量

large quantities of 大量的

shipment quantity 够装运的数量

We can supply any reasonable quantity of this merchandise. 对这种商品我们能供应任何适当的数量。

Quantities of green tea have been exported. 曾有大批绿茶出口。

If you cannot arrange entire quantity, please offer us at least half. 如果你们不能足量供货, 至少报给我们半数。

We are prepared to purchase a shipment quantity of this material. 我们准备购买数量够一次装运的这种产品。

14. L/C 信用证

L/C 是 letter of credit 的缩略形式。

irrevocable L/C at sight 不可撤销的即期信用证

L/C at sight 即期信用证, 也可写作 sight L/C

L/C available by draft at 30 days after sight 凭 30 天远期汇票付款的信用证

30 days time/term L/C 见票后30天议付的信用证

15. draft

n. 汇票

sight draft 即期汇票，也可写作 draft at sight

payable by sight draft 凭即期汇票支付

16. CIF 到岸价

CIF=cost, insurance and freight，成本加保险加运费报价。CIF是价格术语的一种。

17. minimum order quantity 起订量或最小订购量，缩写为 MOQ

The MOQ is 500 pcs. 起订量是500件。

18. delivery

n. 交货

effect/make delivery 交货

take delivery 提货

delivery date 交货日期

关于交货日期的其他表述有：time of delivery, delivery time

delivery order（D/D）提货单

We will take delivery of the goods as soon as they are released from the Customs. 一俟海关放行我们即将货物提出。

19. effect

v. 实施；实行；实现；*n.* 实施，生效；结果，效果；财物

in effect 实际上；有效的

take effect 开始生效

with effect from 自……生效，自……实行

We shall effect shipment without delay. 我方将迅速安排装运。

Please effect the following insurance against WPA. 请办理投保水渍险。

Payment is to be effected by L/C. 以信用证方式付款。

This situation has adverse effects upon us. 这种情况给我方带来不良后果。

The whole company is her personal effects. 整个公司都是她的财产。

The agent agreement will take effect from Jan. 1. 代理协议将于1月1日起生效。

Price is increased 5% with effect from January. 价格自1月份以来上涨了5%。

20. pcs

pcs是pieces的缩略形式，单数为piece，缩写为pc.；数量词，意为只、件、条等。

21. custom

n. 习惯，惯例

It is our custom to trade on the basis of L/C. 我方惯例是以信用证方式交易。

22. as per 根据，按照

as per list price 按照表上价格

as per enclosed documents 根据所附单据

As per your request，we have marked the cases with gross，tare and net weight. 我方已按贵方要求在箱上注明毛重、皮重及净重。

We handle a wide of light industrial products as per list enclosed. 我公司经营多种轻工业产品，详见附表。

23. turnover

n. 成交量；营业额；货物周转率

We sell goods at low prices for a quick turnover. 我们低价销售以期快速周转。

24. O/A 记账；赊销

O/A 是 open account 的缩略形式，是一种付款方式。

25. T/T 电汇

T/T 是 telegraphic transfer 的缩略形式；电汇是汇付的一种。

We accept payment by T/T or L/C. 我们接受电汇或信用证支付。

3.6 Useful Sentences 实用语句

1. Here is our inquiry list. You'll find the required items, specifications and quantities all there.

这是我们的询价单。 所需要的品种、规格和数量都在上面。

2. I'm especially interested in Art No. 4 and No.5. Can you quote on them?

我对 4 号货和 5 号货尤其感兴趣。 您能报给我这两种规格的价格么？

3. Please inform us the quantity that can be supplied from stock.

请告知可提供现货的数量。

4. We would like to have you best price CIF New York, including your commission.

我方想知道贵方的包含佣金在内的纽约到岸价。

5. Please state your best terms and discount for cash.

请告知以现金支付的优惠条件和折扣比例。

6. We would like to know what you offer as well as your sales conditions of this line.

我们想了解一下你方这款产品的供应能力和销售条件。

7. Please send us samples and quote us your lowest prices FOB Ningbo for the listed items.

请贵方寄来清单上所列货物的样品并报最低的宁波离岸价。

8. We would also like to the minimum export quantities per color and per design.

我方还想了解各类商品的每种颜色和花样的最低出口起订量。

9. We have seen your advertisement in *China Daily* and shall be glad if you will send us particulars of bed sheets and pillowcases.

我们在《中国日报》上看到你们的广告，敬请告知有关床单和枕套的详细情况。

10. May I have a price list with specification?

能给我一份包含多种规格的价格单么？

11. According to your questions, pls find my reply as follows.

按照您提出的问题，我的回复如下。

12. Our new price list is being prepared and will be sent to you soon.

我们的新价格表正在准备中，后续即可发送。

13. As a rule, we could only do T/T or L/C at sight.

作为惯例，我们只接受电汇或者即期信用证。

14. Our main market is the USA, and turnover is roughly 5 million USD per year.

我们的主要市场是美国，年销售额大约500万美元。

15. I have to check with my vendor about the updated price.

我需要跟我的供应商确认一下新的价格。

16. Please find our updated price list for our beauty cases in attachment.

关于我公司的化妆箱，请看附件更新过的报价表。

17. Would you like to evaluate our samples in advance?

您想先看看我们的样品吗？

18. We can usually deliver within four weeks of receiving an order.

通常我们在收到订单后4周内供货。

19. Thank you for your inquiry of March 5 on textiles.

感谢您3月5日关于纺织品的询盘。

20. It is better for us to handle the full container order.

对我们来说，操作整柜的订单更好。

3.7 Exercises 练习

I Translate the following words and expressions into English or Chinese.

1. 特别折扣

2. 价格表

3. 数量

4. 到岸价

5. 付款方式

6. specific inquiry

7. updated price

8. transaction cost

9. MOQ

10. L/C

Key 3.1

II Choose the best answer.

1. Please inform us_____delivery date and payment terms.

A. in　　　　　　B. on　　　　　C. at　　　　　D. of

2. We confirm_____accepted your proposal yesterday.

A. have　　　　　B. having　　　C. to have　　　D. has been

3. Our company acts_____the sole agent for your products.

A. for　　　　　　B. on　　　　　C. as　　　　　D. under

4. Some samples will be sent_____request.

A. at　　　　　　B. on　　　　　C. for　　　　　D.in

5. I have to check _____ my vendor about the updated price.

A. with　　　　　B. to　　　　　C. on　　　　　D. at

6. The letter we sent last week is an enquiry_____color TV sets.

A. about　　　　　B. for　　　　　C. of　　　　　D. as

7. We should be pleased to send you some samples of our new cell phones on approval, _____our own expense.

A. at　　　　　　B. on　　　　　C. for　　　　　D. in

8. Please send us your price list _____ our reference.

A. in　　　　　　B. on　　　　　C. at　　　　　D. for

9. Have read your email _____March 3.

A. about　　　　　B. for　　　　　C. of　　　　　D. as

10. Pls let me know if you are interested _____ some of the items.

A. at　　　　　　B. on　　　　　C. for　　　　　D. in

III　Translate the following sentences into English or Chinese.

1. 报价单会在本周五之前发给您。

2. 我们对贵方在这次广交会上展列的机械玩具感兴趣，请详细告知出口条件。

3. 你们的报价都是成本加运费加保险的到岸价，我们希望你们能报离岸价。

4. 我们有经验操作贴牌生产的订单。

5. 除非另有规定或经双方同意，所有价格都是不含佣金的净价。

6. To produce them will cost about 20 days. To send them until arrival in Sydney about 20 days.

7. Attached some photos for your review, for our hot-selling items.

8. Please let us know what you can offer in this line as well as your sales terms, such as mode of payment, time of delivery, discount.

9. We're one of the largest machine importers in Canada. We used to buy machine from Japan, but now we are expanding into China.

10. We would appreciate it if you let us know whether you allow cash or trade discount.

IV Translate the following body of the letter into English.

我方非常高兴收到贵方6月5日的询盘。现随函附上图文目录和价格表,以提供贵方所需的详情。 同时,我方另行邮寄了一些样品,相信贵方检验之后,会认可这是一批质优价廉的货物。

对于每种购买数量不少于500打的产品,我方给予2%的折扣,以即期信用证支付。

因为柔软且耐用,我们的棉布床单和枕套越来越畅销。目前,我方的产品供不应求。但如果贵方不晚于月底订货,我方会确保立即装运。

V Writing task.

Write a letter as per the following background and information.

客户Mike要求我们根据他寄送过来的样品材质报价。但收到样品后,发现这个样品的材料不是ABS而是PP,因此,工厂是需要重新核算价格的。

主管让你先给客户回一封邮件,告诉他:寄送的样品收到并已经转交工厂了,但是因为材料不同,工厂需要重新核算价格,但让他放心,我们会尽快报价的。 同时跟客户强调一下近期国内原材料涨价,希望一旦价格确定后能够尽快确认交易,以便我们及时采购原材料并安排生产。

VI Comprehensive practical training.

1. Read the following inquiry and try to analyze it with your partner.

2. Write a reply to the inquiry as per the business background and information.

（1）经过跟主管请示和同事沟通,得知公司是可以提供免费样品的,但需要客户支付运费。到美国的快递费大概50美元,一般建议西联汇款。

（2）主管交代你回复客户的询盘时,可以推荐一下目前促销的新品(随附小册子的项目3号),也可以给客户顺便寄送两个新品的样品。

Subject: Inquiry for Razors

Hello

My name is Ian. I am looking to buy a bulk order of razors. Probably around 50,000. I would like to get some samples to test the quality of the razor first.

Can you send me some samples? I will pay for the shipping and the razor cost.

Thank you.

Ian

3.8 Supplement & Extension 补充与拓展

价格术语

价格术语（price terms）也称为贸易术语（trade terms），是在长期的国际贸易实践中产生的，用简短的英文缩写字母来表示商品的价格构成，说明交易地点，确定买卖双方的风险、责任，以及费用划分等问题的专门用语。

目前，由国际商会制定并广泛使用的对国际贸易术语进行统一解释的惯例有Incoterms 2000 和 Incoterms® 2010，最新版本是 Incoterms® 2020。以下解释以 Incoterms® 2010版本为准。

一、仅适用于海运及内河水运的三种主要贸易术语

（一）FOB术语

Free on Board（insert named port of shipment）——船上交货（插入指定装运港），是指当出口商在指定的装运港将货物运至进口商指定的船上，即完成交货。

（二）CFR术语

Cost and Freight（insert named port of destination）——成本加运费（插入指定目的港），是指出口商需签订将货物从装运港运至指定目的港的运输合同，支付货物运至指定目的港所需的运费和必要的费用，并在装运港将货物装到船上，即完成交货义务。

（三）CIF术语

Cost, Insurance and Freight（insert named port of destination）——成本、保险费加运费（插入指定目的港），是指出口商需签订将货物从装运港运至指定目的港的运输合同，支付货物运至指定目的港所需的运费和必要的费用，同时还需为货物办理在运输途中的保险，并在装运港将货物装到船上，即完成交货义务。

3种贸易术语的异同点如下。

相同点有6项。

1. 交货地点相同。3种贸易术语的交货地点都在装运港的船上。

2. 风险划分的界限相同。3种贸易术语中买卖双方风险的转移都以货物在装运港装上船为界限，卖方承担货物装上船为止的一切风险，买方承担货物装上船之后的一切风险。

3. 适用的运输方式相同。3种贸易术语都适用于海运或内河运输，不适用于陆运、空运或多式联运。

4. 出、进口清关手续办理者相同。3种贸易术语的出口清关手续都是由出口商办理，进口清关手续都由进口商办理。

5. 合同性质相同。3种贸易术语的合同都属于装运合同。

6. 交货性质相同。3种贸易术语成交，其成交性质均属于象征性交货。

不同点主要表现在买卖双方承担的责任及费用不同。FOB术语由买方负责租船订舱，支付运费和办理货运保险、支付保费；CFR和CIF术语由卖方负责租船订舱和支付运费；

CIF术语下,卖方还应负责办理货运保险和支付保险费用。

二、适用于任何运输方式的三种主要贸易术语

（一）FCA术语

Free Carrier（insert named place of delivery）——货交承运人（插入指定交货地点），是指出口商在指定的交货地点将货物交给进口商指定的承运人,并办理出口清关手续,即完成交货义务。

（二）CPT术语

Carriage Paid to（insert named place of destination）——货交承运人（插入指定目的地），是指出口商在约定地点（如果当事人间约定了交货地点）向其指定的承运人或其他人交货,但出口商还必须订立货物运至指定目的地的运输合同并支付运费。

（三）CIP术语

Carriage and Insurance Paid to（insert named place of destination）——运费、保险费付至（插入指定目的地），是指出口商在约定地点（如果当事人间约定了交货地点）向其指定的承运人或其他人交货,出口商还需订立货物运至指定目的地的运输合同并支付运费,同时还必须办理货物在运输途中的保险。

3种贸易术语的异同点如下。

相同点有6项。

1. 交货地点相同。3种贸易术语的交货地点都在指定交货地点。

2. 风险划分的界限相同。3种贸易术语中买卖双方风险的转移都以货交承运人为界限。

3. 适用的运输方式相同。3种贸易术语都适用于任何运输方式,也可用于多式联运。

4. 出、进口清关手续办理者相同。三种贸易术语的出口清关手续都由出口商办理,进口清关手续都由进口商办理。

5. 合同性质相同。3种贸易术语的合同都属于装运合同。

6. 交货性质相同。3种贸易术语下的成交,其成交性质均属于象征性交货。

不同点主要表现在买卖双方承担的责任及费用不同。FCA贸易术语下,进口商负责订立运输协议和支付运费;CPT和CIP贸易术语下,出口商负责订立运输协议和支付运费;CIP贸易术语下,出口商还应负责办理货运保险和支付保费。

三、其他贸易术语

（一）EXW术语

EX Works（insert named place of delivery）——工厂交货（插入指定地点），是指当出口商在其所在地（如工厂或仓库）将货物交给进口商处置时,即完成交货责任。

（二）FAS术语

Free alongside Ship（insert named port of shipment）——船边交货（插入指定装运港），是指当出口商在指定的装运港将货物交到进口商指定船的船边（如码头或驳船）,即完成

交货。

（三）DAT术语

Delivered at Terminal (insert named terminal at port or place of destination)——运输终端交货（插入指定目的港或目的地的运输终端），是指当出口商在指定港口或目的地的指定终端将已从运输工具上卸载下来（unload）的货物交给进口商处置时，即完成交货。

（四）DAP术语

Delivered at Place (insert named place of destination)——目的地交货（插入指定目的地），是指当出口商在指定目的地将运输工具上准备卸载的货物（ready for unloading）交给进口商处置时，即完成交货。

（五）DDP术语

Delivered Duty Paid (insert named place of destination)——完税后交货（插入指定目的地），是指当出口商在指定目的地将已办理进口清关手续的在运输工具上尚未卸下的货物交给进口商处置时，即完成交货。

Incoterms®2010贸易术语对比如表3.1所示。

表3.1　Incoterms® 2010 贸易术语对比

类别	国际代码	术语名称（英文名称）	术语名称（中文名称）	交货地点	风险转移点	报关责任费用（出口）	报关责任费用（进口）	运输费用	保险费用	交货运输状态
适用于任何运输方式	EXW	EX Works (insert named place of delivery)	工厂交货（插入指定交货地点）	商品所在地或产地	在指定地点交由进口商处置时	进口商	进口商	进口商	进口商	不装上进口商备妥车辆
	FCA	Free Carrier (insert named place of delivery)	货交承运人（插入指定交货地点）	出口国仓库、车站、机场、码头	承运人或运输代理人处置货物后	出口商	进口商	进口商	进口商	当地要装装异地不卸承运人运输工具
	CPT	Carriage Paid to (insert named place of destination)	货交承运人（插入指定目的地）	出口国仓库、车站、机场、码头	承运人或运输代理人处置货物后	出口商	进口商	出口商	进口商	当地要装装异地不卸承运人运输工具
	CIP	Carriage and Insurance Paid to (insert named place of destination)	运费、保险费付至（插入指定目的地）	出口国仓库、车站、机场、码头	承运人或运输代理人处置货物后	出口商	进口商	出口商	出口商	当地要装装异地不卸承运人运输工具
	DAT	Delivered at Terminal (insert named terminal at port or place of destination)	运输终端交货（插入指定目的港或目的地的运输终端）	目的港、地的承运人运输终端	抵达目的地的运输工具上卸下交由进口商处置时	出口商	进口商	出口商	出口商	要从运输工具上卸下
	DAP	Delivered at Place (insert named place of destination)	目的地交货（插入指定目的地）	指定目的地	抵达目的地的运输工具上，且已做好卸载准备时	出口商	进口商	出口商	出口商	不从运输工具上卸下
	DDP	Delivered Duty Paid (insert named place of destination)	完税后交货（插入指定目的地）	指定目的地	抵达目的地的运输工具上，且已做好卸载准备时	出口商	出口商	出口商	出口商	不从运输工具上卸下
适用于海运及内河水运	FAS	Free alongside Ship (insert named port of shipment)	船边交货（插入指定装运港）	指定的装运港	货物到达船边	出口商	进口商	进口商	进口商	置于码头或驳船上
	FOB	Free on Board (insert named port of shipment)	船上交货（插入指定装运港）	指定的装运港	货物装上船	出口商	进口商	进口商	进口商	装上指定船舶
	CFR	Cost and Freight (insert named port of destination)	成本加运费（插入指定目的港）	装运港	货物装上船	出口商	进口商	出口商	进口商	装上指定船舶
	CIF	Cost, Insurance and Freight (insert named port of destination)	成本、保险费加运费（插入指定目的港）	装运港	货物装上船	出口商	进口商	出口商	出口商	装上指定船舶

Chapter 4

Offers & Quotations

发盘与报价专题
——细致准确，体现专业

学习目标

☆知识目标

✓了解虚盘和实盘的区别；

✓掌握不同种类发盘信的特点和回复要点；

✓掌握发盘信、还盘信、报价信和还价函的内容结构；

✓掌握发盘与报价专题常用词句。

☆能力目标

✓能够运用所学知识并结合不同场景撰写发盘信、还盘信、报价信及还价函；

✓能够对客户的还价做出合理和适当的回复。

4.1 Introduction 知识介绍

4.1.1 商务知识

报价专题学习内容包括：了解实盘和虚盘，撰写发盘信、还盘信和反还盘信。

按照交易磋商的4个环节（询盘—发盘—还盘—接受），在询盘之后，就是发盘了。发盘（offer）也称报盘、发价、报价（quotation），是指买方或卖方向对方提出的各项交易条件。发盘可以是应对方询盘的要求发出的，也可以是在没有询盘的情况下，直接向对方发出。在国际贸易实务中，发盘一般是由卖方在收到来自买方的具体询盘信后发出的，但也可以由买方发出，称为递盘（bid）。

发盘是有实盘和虚盘之分的。实盘（firm offer）在法律上被称为"要约"，除了要有完整和明确的交易条件外，还要有明确的有效期。在有效期内，如果买方接受了实盘，则卖方必须按照实盘信的交易内容达成交易。虚盘（non-firm offer）是卖方给出的参考交易条件，一般没有明确的有效期，不具备法律约束力。

在接到发盘后，受盘方应对报盘的内容进行认真研究。如果受盘人认为发盘信中的价格或者其他的交易条件不满意，可以拒绝接受，也可以向发盘人提出修改建议，这种对发盘内容进行修改或变更的表示就是还盘（counter-offer），在法律上称为"反要约"。还盘实际上是受盘人以发盘人的身份发出的一个新盘，此时，原发盘人成为新的受盘人。一旦提出还盘，原发盘即告失效，原发盘人不再受其约束。对还盘再次提出修改意见称为反还盘（counter-counter-offer）。在实际业务中，还盘与返还盘可以在双方之间反复进行，直到双方完全同意对方的交易条件，达成交易。

4.1.2 信函结构

发盘信的正文内容结构一般包括3项。

（1）对对方的来函或询盘表示感谢。

（2）发盘的具体内容。这部分要涵盖以价格为核心的主要交易条件，如品名、质量、数量、包装、单价、运输和支付等。

（3）明确发盘性质，是实盘还是虚盘。如果是实盘，需要说明有效期。如果是虚盘，则一般有如下的表述方法：subject to our final confirmation（以我方最后确认为准），或者subject to the goods being unsold（以货物未售出为准）。

实盘所列的交易条件必须明确、完整，不能含糊，不可让对方在阅读后感觉还有很多不清楚之处。实盘在规定有效期时，要明确规定此期限的起止日期和地点，避免误解。

还盘信的正文内容结构一般包括3项。

（1）表示感谢。

（2）明确不能接受的交易条件，如价格或其他交易条件，并适当陈述原因。例如，同其他供应商相比价格太高，交货期太迟错过销售季节等。

（3）提出解决方案和建议，也就是新的交易条件。

4.2 Task and Project 任务和项目

Task 1：了解发盘信，区分虚盘和实盘

☞ 业务背景与任务

　　ABC公司进出口部，收到以下两封发盘信。

例4-1：发盘信1

Subject：Offer for Laser Printer

Dear Mike,

As requested in your email of April 20. We offer as follows:

Commodity: 500 sets of Laser Printer, ZY630,

Color: White

Packing: in carton, 1 set/carton

Price: US$ 50 per set CIF Sydney

Shipment: within 45 days after receipt of your L/C

Payment: By 100% L/C at sight

This offer is firm, your reply should reach us no later than May 20.

Regards,

Monica Wang

例4-2：发盘信2

Subject：Offer for Laser Printer

Dear Mike,

Thank you for your inquiry. We offer as follows:

Commodity: Laser Printer, ZY630,

Color: White/Black

Packing: in carton, 1 set/carton
Price: US$ 50 per set FOB Ningbo

This offer is subject to our final confirmation.

Regards,

Monica Wang

Notes
1. offer：发盘，报盘
2. laser printer：激光打印机
3. packing：包装
4. carton：纸箱
5. firm offer：实盘
6. non-firm offer：虚盘
7. subject to our final confirmation：以我方最后确认为准

☞ 讨论与分析任务
　　请两人一组讨论并分析：哪一个是实盘？哪一个是虚盘？并概述原因。

Task 2：撰写发盘信

☞ 业务背景和任务
　　宁波3A外贸公司在9月20日收到加拿大JY公司的邮件（发信人为John Smith），在信中对3A公司目前的新产品KKK手机进行了询盘，拟购数量为400个，所选规格为E680，要求提供CIF温哥华报价，以及告知折扣、支付和交货期等情况。
　　其他信息参考：单价600美金，收到订单后一个月内可发货，订购500个以上有3%折扣，即期信用证支付，发盘一周内有效。

☞ 写作任务
　　请以3A公司业务员的身份，结合上述内容撰写实盘信进行回复。

例4-3：卖方发出的实盘信

Subject：A Firm Offer for E680 Mobile Phone
Dear John,

Thank you for your inquiry of September 20, in which you required about the details of our products, newly developed KKK E680.

We are pleased to make you the following firm offer, subject to your reply reaching us within 7 days from today.

Commodity: KKK mobile phone

Specification: E680

Quantity: 400 pieces

Price: at US$ 600 per piece, CIF Vancouver

Color: black, white, blue

Shipment: within 30 days after the order

Payment: by irrevocable L/C payable by draft at sight

On orders for 500 pieces or more, we will allow a special discount of 3%.

We are hopefully expecting your order and please be assured that it will receive our prompt attention.

Best regards,

Monica

Notes

1. mobile phone：手机

2. commodity：商品

3. specification：规格

　　卖方收到来自买方的具体询盘信，对此进行回复，这就是发盘。在这封篇幅为四段的发盘信中，第一段对买方的询盘表示感谢，提到了对方询盘的日期和所询产品的具体信息，以便唤起对方记忆，迅速定位。第二段是报盘内容：首先明确了该发盘的性质和有效期，然后是具体内容，涵盖了以价格为核心的基本交易条款，明确且具体。第三段是关于数量折扣的说明，一句话独立成段。第四段是结尾段，表示卖方对订单的期待和回复的关注。整个发盘信的结构清晰，难易适中，便于学习和借鉴。

　　实盘是有约束力的发盘，发盘人在有效期内不能随意变更或撤销。与虚盘相比较，实盘更容易受到受盘人的重视，有利于双方迅速达成交易。发盘人在做出发盘前，必须对发盘价格、交易条件进行认真的核算和分析，确保发盘内容的准确，以免因对市场情况估计有误而陷入被动。

Task 3：撰写还盘信

☞ *业务背景和任务*

    加拿大JY家公司的John Smith在9月22日收到宁波3A公司的发盘后，对单价做出了还盘，希望降价3%，其他交易条件表示接受。

☞ *写作任务*

    请以JY公司John Smith的身份，结合上述内容撰写还盘信。

例4-4：买方的还盘信

Subject：A Counter Offer for E680 Mobile Phone

Dear Monica,

Thank you for your offer of September 22 for E680 Mobile Phone.

In reply, we regret to state that your price has been on the high side. As you know, the price of similar goods made in other countries has been 5% lower than that of yours.

Admittedly, the quality of your products is slightly higher, but the price is also higher so that we can not get much profit. To set up a long term relationship, we hope you can cut down your price by 3%.

As the market is competitive, we hope you will consider our counter-offer most favorable and we hope to hear from you soon.

Best regards,

John

Notes

1. counter offer：还盘
2. on the high side：(指价格) 偏高
3. profit：利润

    这是一封买方撰写的还盘信，全文四段，篇幅适中。首段用一句话对卖方的报盘表示感谢，且提到了原发盘日期和产品，以确定双方沟通主题。第二段直接提出因价格高而无法接受，并给出了同业竞争性价格对比作为佐证。第三段是两句话，首先表示对卖方所供商品质量的认可，接着又再次说明不能接受报价的原因，然后顺势提出解决方案。第四段是结尾段，买方以市场竞争化态势为依据，表示对卖方接受还盘的督促和期待。

这封还盘信，结构清晰，表意连贯，递进性强，便于学习者掌握还盘信的基本结构，了解撰写还盘信的一些技巧和具体应用。在国际贸易业务中，由于买卖双方各自立场不同，都想说服对方接受自己的意见。因此，发盘之后是还盘，还盘之后是返还盘，返还盘后是再还盘……一笔生意，往往要经过几个轮次反复的还盘，才能最终成交。

Task 4: 撰写返还盘信

☞ **业务背景和任务**

宁波3A公司，在9月24日收到加拿大JY公司John Smith的还盘后，认为己方的产品质量好，所报的价格已经是优惠价，若再降价就无法保证质量了。因此，去函拒绝降价，希望对方能够理解，并期盼收到订单。

☞ **写作任务**

请以3A公司业务员的身份，结合上述内容撰写返还盘信。

例4-5: 卖方的返还盘

Subject: Reply to Your Counter Offer for E680 Mobile Phone

Dear John,

We note from your email of Sept.24 that you are not satisfied with the price.

We very regret to say that our products are of high quality and unique design, and the price has always been accepted by other companies. Such being the case, we feel very sorry to say that we can't cut our price to guarantee the good quality and the novel design. And in fact, we have offered you the most favorable price.

We hope you may reconsider it and we sincerely hope that we can receive your order soon.

Best regards,

Monica

Notes

novel: 新奇的；新颖的

在这封返还盘中，卖方给出三个理由来支撑报价的合理性：其一，产品的高质量和独特的设计；其二，价格被广泛认可和接受；其三，所报价格是最优惠价。这三个理由放在同一段来汇总陈述，增加了说服力度。

买方的还盘，同时也是一个新的发盘。而卖方在收到还盘后，对其提出修改意见，这个被称为反还盘（或返还盘）。无论在还盘还是反还盘信中，对己方不能接受的交易条件，要有明确的表示，不能模糊不清。同时在拒绝对方某项交易条件时也要保持礼貌，并且要给出合理的理由，以维持对方商谈的兴趣。

4.3 Actual Case Letters 实战信函

发盘和还盘是买卖双方就目标商品的各项交易条件进行磋商。实际业务中，这个磋商的焦点往往是非常集中的，就是价格。通常情况下，买方会同时向不同国家的不同卖主询价，以便取得价格信息，了解某种商品的行情，而卖方对此进行回复的信函也被称为报价函（quotation）。

严格地讲，报价函和发盘信是有区别的。报价函对卖方没有约束力，买方也不需要对每个报价函都作出答复。但在实际业务中，有时报价函中既有交易条件，又有有效期限，等同于实盘。以报价函替代发盘信是外贸业务中常见的做法。以下几篇报价函及还价函，均来自外贸业务实践，结合教学目标和商业保密原则略做调整和修改，以方便学习者学习和参考。

例4-6：卖方发出的报价函1

Subject：Quote Sheet for Portable Beauty Machines

Hi Mike,

Thank you for your inquiry for portable beauty machines. The quotation is as follows:

Name: Portable Beauty Machines, Item No. CM-4,
Qty: 200pcs
Price: FOB Ningbo, USD 23/pc
Packing: 1pc/giftbox, 20 pcs/carton, Carton size: 53 cm×41 cm×40 cm
Weight: about 15.5 kg

As to the box, the gift box is white without any logo. For the quantity of 200 pcs, we don't make them with your logo or brand. But it's can be discussed in a way.

If any questions, please contact me freely.

Regards,

Monica Wang

Notes

1. portable beauty machines：便携式美容仪
2. giftbox：礼盒
3. weight：重量
4. logo：标识，标记，徽标

　　这封报价函是将报价细节写入信函的正文中，全文四段，呈纺锤形结构。首尾段各用一句话来开篇和结束，主体为中间两个段落。其中第二段是具体的报价信息，包括品名、型号、数量、价格和包装等内容。第三段是单独对货物的包装盒和logo刷制进行了说明和解释。"the gift box is white without any logo" 这里不是强调包装盒的颜色是白色，而是表示该货物为中性包装。中性包装的意思是：包装上不显示任何标识，没有产地和国别等信息。

　　一般情况下，报价函有两种方式，一种是直接在邮件正文里注明价格和相关参数，另一种就是制作报价单随函发送。特别是对于大客户、专业客户和很多中小客户来说，他们都是需要报价单的。报价单不仅能让人看起来一目了然，而且也方便对方做参考比较。

例4-7：卖方发出的报价函2

Subject：Quotation Sheet for Led Strips

Hi Mike,

Thank you for your reply of March 10.

The attachment is our quotation, please check it.

You can be certain that our price is really competitive. Kindly let me know if any other questions.

Regards,

Monica

Encl: Quotation sheet for LED strips.

Notes

1. quotation sheet：报价单
2. LED strips: LED灯条

这是一个关于LED灯条的报价函，具体报价细节是以附件形式随附的，全文是三段论，共四句话，内容简洁且结构清晰。这种以随附报价单的形式发送的报价函是目前进出口业务中较为常见的。在多数公司，都有固定的报价单模板，可以按照客户要求和业务信息填写好后放入附件即可。这类报价信函，就信函本身而言，是很容易掌握和模仿的。但是，随附的报价单是一个公司或者这个业务员专业性的体现，需要格外重视。

无论是随同发送报价单附件的形式，还是直接将报价细节写入正文，报价函的写作内容都可以概括为以下三点。(1)表示感谢。建议提到来函的日期或者主题。(2)报价信息。这部分具体有两种做法：可以是简单的文字＋随附报价单，也可以直接在邮件中详细列明报价细节。在实际业务中，结合公司的具体操作习惯即可。(3)其他信息。这部分的目的是促进客户回复或接受，也可以是针对报价单中的内容做进一步的解释和说明。

例4-8：卖方的还价信1

Subject：Grease Gun Pricing

Dear Mike，

I'm so sorry that we couldn't meet your target of USD 5.3/pc with color box.

As I mentioned in my previous mail, our price was based on the different packing method.

视频4.3

Anyway, we could reduce our margin to establish our business. Our final price is USD 5.5 with a color box, and USD 5.2 with a poly bag.

If you'd like to do promotion for this item, we suggest you confirm the poly bag instead. According to our experience, other customers mainly use this simple packaging for EU market.

Please help to check with buyer and give me reply soon.

Regards,

Monica Wang

Notes
1. grease gun pricing: 黄油枪价格磋商

2. target: 目标

3. target price: 目标价格

3. previous: 之前的，先前的

4. packing method: 包装方式

5. EU market: 欧盟市场

6. poly bag: 塑料袋包装

从这封信的内容分析，我们可以判断，写信人的策略是：进退有度，适当妥协。写作的思路则是：先抑后扬。首先明确地告知对方，你们的目标价是不能被接受的。紧接着就跟进解释，不能接受的缘由。再接下来是转折，提出让步和解决方案。紧接着又马上跟进，说明这个方案的可行性。最后简洁地结尾。全文环环相扣，一气呵成，是一篇值得反复体会和学习的实战案例还价信。

在这封还价信发出后，买方接受了么？当然没有，生意哪有这么容易做。在这封信函发出一周后，买方回复了一封新的还价信。在信中，罗列了各种理由，仍然坚持原来的目标价格，要求卖方让步。基于此，卖方撰写了下面的还价信2。

例4-9：卖方的还价信2

Subject: Final Price for Grease Gun

Dear Mike,

To be frank with you, we have no margin to reduce the pricing again.

In fact, the price is very important to win this order, but the quality counts for much more. We couldn't debase our quality level to achieve your price aim. I'm sorry.

I have discussed with our top manager, and decided to proceed in below suggestions.

1. USD 5.50/pc, with color box packaging, based on 10,000 pcs.

2. USD 5.20/pc, with simple poly bag packaging, based on 10,000 pcs.

3. 3% will be provided as a special discount, when quantity up to 30,000 pcs.

Please help to consider and inform us which way is better for you. We understand that you have to test your local market and retail price. And we're pleased to do a trial order for you with small quantity in our first business. Maybe 5,000–8,000 pcs are workable for you to make a decision, with no price increase.

Regards,

Monica Wang

Notes

1. to be frank with you: 坦白地说
2. quality counts for much more: 质量更重要
3. retail price: 零售价
4. trial order: 试订单

这封还价函的内容和层次感更为丰富,构思的思路依然是先抑后扬。首先是否定和简要的原因解释,接着就提出解决方案,最后跟进做了另一个角度的让步。整体行文流畅,言辞恳切,同时有理有据,让对方很难拒绝。

4.4 Summary 小结

视频4.4

发盘是交易一方提出交易条件,表示按此条件达成交易的行为,发盘有实盘和虚盘之分。还盘是受盘人收到发盘后,不能完全同意对方的交易条件而提出的不同建议。由于价格是交易条件的核心,在实际业务中,发盘也被称为报价,还盘也被称为还价。

本章以出口业务为主导,展示并分析了9封发盘、还盘、报价和还价相关信函。所选信函突出出口商视角,侧重交易磋商技能养成,通过样函展示和撰写思路分析,培养学习者的商务思维和地道表达。

发盘和还价信写作的注意事项如下。

1. 发盘和报价的区别

发盘也称报盘、发价、报价,但严格讲,发盘和报价是有区别的。在国际贸易中,各国用法并不统一,客户各自表意习惯也有不同。因此,应根据信函具体内容进行分析和判断。

2. 发盘信的撰写

发盘有实盘和虚盘之分。实盘的发盘人有订立合同的意图,且受发盘内容的约束。虚盘是参考性交易条件,被视为一般的业务联系,是不受约束的发价。

在日常业务中,实盘所列的交易条件必须肯定、明确、完整,一般应包括品名、规格、数量、包装、单价、运输和支付条件等,同时应说明有效期限。建议有效期以3~5天为宜,且需明确规定此期限的起止日期和地点,以免造成误解。

虚盘一般需注明 "for your reference"(仅供参考) 或 "subject to our final confirmation"(以我方最后确认为准) 等保留或限制性条件,以明示发盘性质。

3. 报价函的撰写

发送报价函有两种方式:一种是直接在邮件正文里注明价格和其他交易条件,另一种是制作报价单随函发送。第一种形式，报价函的正文内容相对较多，第二种形式，因为有报价单随附，因此内容较为简单。一般来说，大客户、专业客户和很多中小客户，都是需要报价单的。报价单不仅能让人看起来一目了然，而且也方便对方做参考比较。

4. 还盘信的撰写

还盘信中拒绝对方某项交易条件时要保持礼貌，并且应给出充分、合理的理由。还盘不一定是还价格，对支付条件、装运期等主要交易条件提出不同建议，也属于还盘。

5. 回复还价函及价格磋商信

在国际贸易中，还盘涉及方方面面。不同的业务、不同的客户，还盘的理由和诉求点也是千差万别的，但价格始终是还盘的核心。收到买方还盘后，业务员需要依靠自己的经验来判断，客户的还价是真实的，还是带有水分的。在回复的时候，则要结合自己对市场和行业的了解，以及公司的具体执行方案，妥善审慎地处理。

回复还价函及价格磋商信的撰写要有针对性，不论是降价还是维持原价，都需要有合理的理由。一味地拒绝，不留余地，或者一味地退让，没有底线，都是不可取的。而在多轮次拉锯战中，要特别谨慎，尤其要注意语气和措辞细节，不能被对方猜出自己的底牌和价格底线。进退有度、有理有据、先抑后扬、适当妥协是交易磋商和价格谈判的有效策略。

4.5 Useful Words & Expressions 实用词汇及短语

1. offer

n. & *v.* 发盘；报盘

make/send/give an offer for... 对……进行报盘

firm offer 实盘

non-firm offer 虚盘

Please make us an offer CIF Ningbo for 500 pairs for ladies shoes. 请按宁波到岸价报给我方500双女鞋的价格。

This offer will remain effective for another 10 days from 20th May. 本报盘有效期为自5月20日起10天。

A Japanese seller has made us an offer at $100 per metric ton. 一日本卖主向我方报价每公吨100美元。

We offer you firm subject to reply by 5 p. m., our time, Tuesday, 9th May. 兹报实盘，以我方时间5月9日周二下午5点以前答复为有效。

2. subject to 以……为条件的；以……为有效的；在……条件下

The offer is subject to our final confirmation. 此报盘以我方最后确认为准。

We make you an offer subject to the goods being unsold. 我方向你方报盘，以未售出为准。

Subject to your shipment in May, we will order 5,000 tons. 如果贵方5月份装运，我方将订购5,000吨。

3. commodity

n. 商品；货物；（尤指国际贸易中的）物品、产品或材料

BBM company has increased prices on several commodities. BBM公司提高了一些商品的价格。

4. counter offer

v. & n. 还盘；还价（也可写作counteroffer 或counter-offer）

We are sorry to tell you that we can not accept your counter-offer. 非常抱歉地告诉您，我方不能接受贵方还价。

The price you counteroffered is not in line with the prevailing market. 贵方的还盘价格与市场价不符。

We counter offer for 1,000 pcs，Ladies Yoga Suits at USD 10.00 per piece FOE Ningbo. 我方还盘1,000件女士瑜伽服，每件10美元，宁波离岸价。

5. on the high side （指价格）偏高

We regret to say that we cannot accept your offer，as your price is found（to be）on the high side. 抱歉地告知由于贵方价格偏高，我方不能接受贵方的报盘。

类似的表述有：

Your price is a bit high. 贵方价格有点高。

Your price is too high. 贵方价格太高。

Your price is rather stiff. 贵方价格相当高。

Your price is excessive. 贵方价格过高。

Your price is prohibitive. 贵方价格令人望而却步。

6. weight

n. 重量

weight memo 重量单

net weight 净重

gross weight 毛重

tare weight 皮重

7. logo

n. 标识，标记，徽标

logo是logotype的缩略形式。

8. quotation

n. 报价；行情

quotation sheet 报价单；价目表

exchange rate quotation 外汇行情

discount quotation 贴现行情

quote

v. 报价

Please quote us your lowest price for walnuts. 请向我方报核桃的最低价。

9. EU market 欧盟市场

10. to be frank with you 坦白地说；直率地说；坦诚相告

11. count for 有价值；有重要性

Quality counts for much more. 质量更为重要。

12. trial order 试订单

Place a trial order with... 向……下试订单

13. stock

v. & n. 储存；备货；现货；存货

We have a large tailoring department and would like to stock a new type of material. 我们公司有个很大的成衣部，想要备置一种新的衣料。

We advise you to stock up while supplies are available. 我们建议你们在供货充足时备置存货。

These are the only stocks available. 这些是仅有的存货。

in stock 有存货；有现货

from stock 可供现货

out of stock 没有库存；无现货

We have 400 metric tons in stock. 我们有400公吨的现货。

We are pleased to inform you that the item you requested can be supplied from stock. 我方很高兴告知贵方，需要的货物有可供应的现货。

We regret that the goods are out of stock now. 很抱歉现在没有现货供应。

stock

adj. 库存的

Stock offers are a touch-and-go kind of things. 现货报盘成交快，一有买主就可立即脱手。

14. charge

v. 收费；索要；把……记账；使承担；指控；使充满

He is charged 5 dollars for mending a pair of shoes. 他修了一双鞋，被索要了5美元。

The new appointed manager is charged with heavy responsibility. 新任命的经理承担了很重的责任。

The Customs charged the company with evasion of taxes. 海关指控该公司逃税。

The battery is charged. 电池被充满电了。

n. 费用；掌管；责任；指控；负荷

Samples will be sent free of charge. 免费寄送样品。

The manager assumes full charge of the business. 经理担负全部经营事务。

The court brought the charge of treason against him. 法院指控他叛国。

chargeable

adj. 可以控诉的；应付费的；应由本人负责的

These expenses are chargeable on him. 这些费用应由他负担。

15. execute

v. 执行；签署

We always do our best to execute our contracts to the full. 我们总是尽可能全面地执行合同。

execution

n. 执行；签署

We hope that you will promptly accept our order and make your usual careful execution. 我们希望贵方迅速接受我方订货，并同往常一样交货时多加注意。

4.6 Useful Sentences 实用语句

1. This offer is firm, your reply should reach us no later than May 20.

此发盘为实盘，贵方请于5月20日前回复。

2. The attachment is our quotation, please check it.

附件是报价单，请查收。

3. Thank you for your inquiry for sth. The quotation is as follows.

感谢贵方对于××的询盘，我们的报价单如下。

4. With reference to your inquiry of July 6, we shall be pleased to supply 100 sets of scanner at the price of $130 each.

感谢您7月6日的询盘，我方很高兴以每台130美元的报价供应100台扫描仪。

5. The prices quoted above are provisional, since we may be compelled by increased costs of raw materials to increase our prices to customers. I will inform you immediately if this happens.

由于原材料的涨价会迫使我方提高产品价格，所以上述报价是暂定价。一旦此类情况发生，我方会马上通知贵方。

6. In view of the goods in great demand, we would advise in your interest that you accept our offer without any delay.

由于商品紧俏，为贵方着想，建议迅速接受我方报盘。

7. Although we appreciate the quality, your price is too high for us to accept.

尽管我们很认可你们的质量，但是这个价格太高了，我们没法接受。

8. In fact, some competitors are quoting a lower price.

实际上，一些竞争者报了更低的价格。

9. If your price is reduced by 10%, we would place a substantial order with you.

如果你能降价10%，我们会下一个大订单。

10. Our survey has confirmed that your price is 5% higher compared with other companies, I'm afraid I have to call the deal off if you can't make any concession.

我方调查证明你方价格和别的公司价格相比高出5%，如果你们不能做些让步，恐怕我方只好放弃这笔交易了。

11. If you have taken everything into consideration, you may find our quotation lowest than those you can get elsewhere.

如果把各种因素都加以考虑，你会发现我们的报价比别处的报价要低。

12. We could reduce our margin to establish our business.

不管怎样，我们就是减少利润也要维持我们之间的业务。

13. We grant a discount of 3% for an order exceeding 1,000 tons.

超过1,000吨我们可以给3%的折扣。

14. As I mentioned in my previous mail, our price was based on the different packing method.

正如我之前邮件中提到的，我们的价格是基于不同的包装方式而变动的。

15. To be frank with you, we have no margin to reduce the pricing again.

坦白地说，我们真的没有再降价的空间了。

16. The price is very important to win this order, but the quality counts for much more.

就这个订单而言，价格是很重要的，但是质量更重要。

17. We couldn't debase our quality level to achieve your price aim.

我们不能以降低我们的质量水准来达到你的价格目标。

18. We are ready to meet you halfway and settle the matter on a 50/50 basis.

我们各让一步，按各让50%的方式解决此问题。

19. I know our price is far exceeds your target, but I still would like to evaluate the sample. I'm sure the quality is different.

我明白我们的报价远远超过您的目标价，但我还是希望您能看一下样品。我保证，品质是完全不同的。

20. We would give you a special discount of 10% if the quantity up to 1×40'HQ.

如果数量可以达到一个40尺高柜，我们可以给您一个10%的特别折扣。

4.7 Exercises 练习

I Translate the following words and expressions into English or Chinese.

1. 以我方最后确认为准
2. 报价单
3. 还盘
4. 质量更为重要
5. 坦白地说
6. EU market
7. business negotiation

🔖 Key 4.1

8. unit price

9. trial order

10. out of stock

II Choose the best answer.

1. We trust that you will find our goods_____.

A. attracting   B. to be attractive   C. attract your attention   D. attractive

2. If the prices are_____, we trust important business are materialize.

A. in line   B. in the line   C. on line   D. on the line

3. We hope you could_____us a special discount of 3% on orders.

A. admit   B. offer   C. send   D. let

4. We have pleasure in enclosing a detailed price list for the goods you_____in your letter.

A. informed   B. said   C. told   D. required

5. If you could increase the_____to 10%, we shall be pleased to buy the complete stock.

A. cost   B. stock   C. discount   D. price

6. This price will remain_____for ten days from the date of letter.

A. valuable   B. invaluable   C. good   D. valid

7.This offer is_____, your reply should reach us no later than May 20.

A. final   B. firm   C. non-firm   D. real

8. This offer is subject_____our final confirmation.

A. to   B. with   C. for   D. on

9.Our price was based_____the different packing method.

A. at   B. upon   C. in   D. on

10.we are offering you goods_____the very high quality.

A. of   B. for   C. at   D. with

III Translate the following sentences into English or Chinese.

1. 如果贵方能订购5,000台,我方将给予10%的折扣。

2.请和您的客户沟通下,并尽快回复我们。

3. 对于现金付款,给予9折优惠。

4.除非你们减价5%,否则我们无法接受报盘。

5. 报价有效期至3月31日止,此日期之后的条款及价格需重新商讨。

6. These quotations are all subject to the fluctuations of the market.

7. 10% discount will be provided if you double the quantity.

8. We have learnt that there is a good demand for wool products in your market, and take this opportunity of enclosing our Quotation Sheet No. 651 for your consideration.

9. We could try a trial order to test the market.

10. Your counter offer is too low and groundless; therefore, it cannot serve as a basis for further negotiation with our manufacturers.

IV Translate the following body of the letter into English.

我方已经收到贵方7月5日的还盘。

但是，贵方建议每双25美元，这对我们来说是太苛刻了。虽然贵方表示以便宜很多的价格即可买到同等质量的鞋子，但是我方坚信我方YR牌3号产品，其质量绝对比同等价位的其他品牌鞋子好。

我方的确很难接受贵方每双25美元的还盘，但是，因为贵方是我们的重要客户，所以我方认为如果贵方至少订购500双，我方可以让步，将价格降至每双30美元。

如贵方及时回复，将不胜感激。

V Writing task.

Write a letter as per the following background and information.

某外贸公司于2月3日收到加拿大ABN公司Mr. Ian Smith的询盘，请根据如下信息撰写实盘信进行回复。

（1）商品：HW手机；（2）规格：HW Mate 10;（3）数量：200打；（4）价格：成本加保险、运费至温哥华单价700美元;（5）装运：收到信用证后一个月内;（6）付款条件：即期信用证;（7）购买量不低于300打的客户有3%折扣;（8）报盘有效期五天。

VI Comprehensive practical training.

Read the following counteroffer and write a reply to the counteroffer as per the business background and information.

1. 对于客户的还价。主管回复：他们只订了500件，怎么打折？ 如果达到1,000件以上，可以考虑给个5%。让你尽量说服客户接受价格或增加订购量。

2. 对于客户想了解运费和保费相关费用的情况。主管让你跟货代和保险公司沟通后，整理好相关费用附上个详单给客户，免得说不清楚。同时叮嘱在这些费用上面，公司一分钱也不要额外增加，以免客户从别的渠道比价后对公司印象不好。

Dear Monica,

Thank you for your offer of May 15 on women's shirts. While appreciating the good quality and design of your shirts, we find your price is rather high for our market, the middle class.

If you can make reduction by 10% discount, we can place the order, 500 pieces.

In addition, we would like to enquire the freight and insurance to Sydney.

Waiting for your reply.

Best regards，

David Smith

4.8 Supplement & Extension 补充与拓展

报价的技巧

报价是一门学问,怎样报价才有效呢? 如何报价既能抓住客户,让客户回复,同时又可以避免被同行从报价中套出信息?

报价的时候,技巧不可或缺。把握客户意向,虚实结合,灵活报价是基本原则。以下报价技巧和应用举例供参考。

一、削弱参照物法

随着互联网的发展,信息透明度越来越高,价格对比成为外贸常态。而这个技巧就是让客户难以找到参照物,使价格没有可比性。

例如,一个太阳能灯,工厂报价每个4元,彩盒包装。这个时候报给客户该怎么报呢? 结合客户的购买意愿和诉求点,报价从0.8美元到8美元,利润从10%到200%之间都可以报。不同的客户,报价是可以不同的。

削弱参照物报价法的应用:不要原封不动按照工厂的数据报出去,而是先给客户提供一些方案。例如,20个产品做一个展示盒,并且提供一个展示盒图片同步发给客户,告诉他这样在超市里摆放会很漂亮,利于销售。或者给客户提供条幅和广告语,将一整套的销售策略做好,等他确定后再酌情报价。

这样一来,价格可比性一下子就被削弱,变得不是那么透明。即使客户拿着这个方案去别处询价,一时也不容易得到非常具体准确的报价。因为展示盒的材质或者促销材料印制工艺不同,价格就会不同,等等。客户在数天之内是很难找到完全等同的参照物的。即便有个别供应商核出来一个低价,客户以此来压价时,也是有回转余地的,或者材质不同,或者再做些更改都是可行的。很可能的情况是客户在找不到什么参照物的情况下,只能凭经验来砍价,然后要么成交,要么没订单。

这种报价的好处是虚虚实实,不怕同行来套价格。这一招要是用得好,效果会很好,不但能提高利润,还能让客户觉得这个供应商很专业,可谓一举两得。

在实际业务中，也有一些供应商在收到询价后，喜欢向客户询问各种信息，想把所有细节弄清楚后再报价，认为这样比较准确和独特。这种想法对终端用户是可行的，但是如果客户也是中间商，就未必会有效了。在外贸业务中，很多国外客户是中间商，他们的终端客户也许只给他一张图，或者简单的一两句描述，其他什么东西都没有。因此他没法给你更多的信息，也没法回答你的若干问题。

这时候，如果有其他供应商给出自己的方案，并给出了建议，客户觉得不错，他可能会把别人的一些参数发给你，让你去核价。这个时候你就头痛了，发现尺寸不是常规的，包装方式也和自己的不一样，材料似乎也有改动，没别的办法，只能让同事和技术部门逐一去核价，结果三催四催，价格报出来还不一定准确。因为这是别人的方案，你被别人牵着鼻子走，自然会很被动。

如果给出方案的那个人是你，那客户拿你的方案去你同行那边询价，这个时候头痛的就是他们了。他们需要根据你设定好的圈子来玩这个游戏，你就牢牢占据了主动位置。所以，报价时不但要给出几套方案，而且速度要快，首先要占据客户的主观思维，让他按照你的游戏规则玩下去。

二、大买家鼓励法

很多客户都知道大买家，同行业当中的大客户和知名客户能让人心生景仰。如果你和大买家有过合作，是不是更能取信你正在开发的潜在客户呢？答案是肯定的。

如果把前面的削弱参照物法和大买家鼓励法合并起来使用，很多时候会有惊人的效果。

假设，有客户就某个产品让你报价，而这个产品系列之前你们同某个知名大买家有过合作。这时候，就可以直接报给客户类似的出货比较好的产品，包括说明书、彩盒设计稿，还有价格和外箱资料等。如果是带有知名大买家logo（商标）的图片，那说服力更强，等于暗示客户：我连某某客户都在做，我们是相当专业的。之后再补充一句："这是我公司之前出货的类似产品，如果您有不同的具体化和差异化需求，我们很乐意帮您询价，或者研究开模生产，请提供进一步的详细资料。"

这就是大买家鼓励法和削弱参照物法的合并操作示例。

对于买家而言，他们只是希望找到合适的供应商来配合他，如果这个供应商还跟他的同行做过，或者和知名买家做过，那就更好了。换位思考一下，如果我们找供应商，不管他是工厂还是贸易公司，首先要衡量的是这个供应商是否足够专业。有些时候，尽管这个供应商的公司或工厂规模不大，但是有好几个国际知名的大公司都曾下单给他，我们就会觉得这家公司很了不起，对产品和热销市场都很熟悉，订单下给他就会比较放心。

三、捆绑策略法

这里所讲的捆绑策略比较特殊，不是把几个产品放在一起捆绑销售，而是利用自己的品牌把自己和客户捆绑起来，让他很难独善其身。

设想，如果他的店里卖的是你的产品，架子上是你的牌子，如果哪天突然要换，消费者会习惯吗?会不会影响他的销售呢?

举例说,比如我们是做文具销售的,那么这个捆绑策略该如何操作呢?

首先,我们可以帮这个买家设计一系列文具类产品的所有纸卡,同时产品给他最低价,条件是他要将该文具一整个系列的订单全部给我,而且要打我们的品牌。我们给他的回报是,所有的纸卡都由同一个工厂做,然后我们另外找包装厂统一包装,这样便不会有色差,而且纸卡的品质都相当接近,客户也会很满意的。那么这样一来,他超市里整个货架的产品都是我们提供的,而且用的是我们的牌子。

几个月以后,我们把其中的一部分产品涨价,客户不接受也得接受,否则一旦他不下其中这几款订单,他的货架就不整齐,就不是统一的纸卡、色调和品牌。这就是我们当初的既定策略,一个集成订单,很多产品我们亏着做,大部分只保住成本,少部分加利润甚至高利润。客户一旦做起来了,半年或一年后,我们就可以把以前亏的那部分全部赚回来,这时候我们就处于主动位置,而客户就比较被动了。

如果客户要终止跟我们的合同,把所有的文具系列换掉,这不是半年一年搞得定的。这个时候我们如果适当地跟客户的买手搞好关系,说服他们,那几乎就没什么问题了,生意可以做得很长久。

有时候,客户可能会问,能不能接受OEM(贴牌生产)或ODM(设计生产)?有没有自己的品牌?这种情况下一定要给出肯定的答复,我们可以贴牌,同时也有自己的品牌。另外,我们也要想办法让客户用我们自己的品牌,这样才能达到捆绑策略的效果。甚至可以考虑给客户适当降一些价格,多给一些优惠,尽量让它选择你的牌子。一旦客户与你同乘一条船,想下来就不是那么容易了。

四、狮子大开口法

如果公司的产品相对比较冷门,竞争的同行不是太多,那不妨试试这个狮子大开口法。但是用这招有个前提,就是你对产品、行情,特别是目标市场有很准确的了解。

对于业务老手来说,这一招是经常会使用的老套路。对于有经验的买家来说,不论你报的价格是高是低,他都会说很高,要求你降价。大部分买家的心理:他们往往买的不是"便宜",而是"占便宜"!

这就像百货商店里有很多服装品牌,一件普通的夏装卖600元,你觉得很贵,等到换季的时候,直接给你打7折,很多朋友明知这个时候没法穿,但是感觉占了便宜,还是会去买,心想买来以后可以放到明年穿,但往往没想到明年自己是不是还会喜欢这件衣服。这个时候,大批的人会把商场挤爆,这就是占便宜的心态。这东西真的便宜吗?未必。市场上很多不是这个牌子的相同款式的衣服,价格可能只有300元不到,但是东西便宜,你不一定会要,你要的是那种占便宜的感觉,这才是很多买家的真正心态。

如果你卖电视机,即使你说one dollar/pc,有经验的买手还是会回答:"Wow, that's too expensive!"这个时候其实更多的是一种博弈,价格已经不再与产品完全挂钩,而更多地取决于谈判的好坏。

只要你的产品够冷门,同行很少,你也知道国外的销售价,这个时候完全可以搞那么一点点差异化，然后报个好价格，静待客户还价，然后再一轮一轮地谈判。谈价格的时候不要害怕会把客户吓走，你不谈又怎么知道不可以呢？

　　以上这些只是报价和谈判过程中一些简单的技巧，但要注意，技巧对于谈判来说只是起到辅助作用，而不是决定作用。商业谈判要以实力为后盾，然后辅之以一些技巧来促成谈判的成功。真正起到决定作用的，还是事先充分的准备、回复的效率、细节的把握，以及对产品和行情的专业度。

Contract Terms: Packing, Shipment, Insurance, Payment and Others

交易细节沟通专题
——坚持底线,持续沟通

学习目标

☆知识目标

✓了解包装、装运、保险、支付等交易细节相关业务背景知识;
✓掌握包装、装运、保险、支付等相关业务沟通信函的内容结构;
✓掌握包装、装运、保险、支付等交易细节专题常用词句。

☆能力目标

✓能够运用所学知识结并合不同场景撰写沟通交易细节的各类信函,包括包装、装运、保险、支付,以及讨论其他细节等;
✓能够对客户关于交易细节相关的信函做出合理和适当的回复。

5.1 Introduction 知识介绍

5.1.1 商务知识

交易细节专题学习内容包括包装（packing）、装运（shipment）、保险（insurance）、支付（payment）、其他细节（others）等5个部分。涉及这些内容的往来函电，一般发生在订单前后。其中一部分是订单确认前的一些交易细节沟通，也有一部分是涉及订单确认后的跟进性业务处理。

1. 包装与标志相关外贸知识

国际流通领域的货物一般要经过长途运输，同时也经常会有转运和储存。进出口双方在签订合同时，应对包装问题进行洽商并做出具体规定。包装相关函电内容主要涉及包装方式、包装材料、唛头和包装费用等，关于此交易条款的沟通主要发生在订单确认前。

在国际贸易中，包装一般分为两类：运输包装（transport packing）和销售包装（selling packing）。运输包装又称大包装或外包装（outer packing），其作用在于保护货物在长时间和远距离的运输过程中不被损坏或丢失，同时，又可方便货物的搬运，起到减少运费、节省租仓和方便计数的作用。销售包装又称小包装和内包装（inner packing），其作用除了保护商品的品质外，还有美化和宣传商品、方便陈列、吸引顾客、促进销售、提高商品价值，以及方便消费者识别、选购、携带和使用的作用。目前，商品的包装呈现向小型化、透明化和实用化发展的趋势。

除以上常规分类外，还有一种中性包装（neutral packing）。这是一种既不标明生产国别、地名和厂名，也不标明原有商标和牌号的包装，甚至在商品内外包装上一个字都没有。采用中性包装的目的是在进口国避税或者满足买方的特别需要。

常见的运输包装：箱，如木箱（wooden case）、铁箱（iron case）、板条箱（crate）、纸箱（carton）等；桶（drum），如木桶（wooden drum）、铁桶（iron drum）、塑料桶（plastic drum）等；包（bale）；袋（bag），如布袋（cloth bag）、麻袋（gunny bag）、纸袋（paper bag）、塑料袋（plastic bag）等；瓶（bottle），如钢瓶（cylinder）、长颈瓶（flask）等；坛（jar）；盒（box）；篓（basket）；托盘（pallet）；集装箱（container）等。此外，也有少数商品不采用包装，仅采取散装和裸装方式。

在商品的外包装上一般会刷有标志。标志类似于人的身份证，进口商和承运人依靠它来区别货物，同时标志也是区别和联系货物与单证关系的手段。包装上的标志信息应与单证上的一致。

标志一般包括运输标志、指示性标志和警告性标志。

运输标志又称唛头（shipping mark），它通常是用模板印制在包装上的标志，由一些简单的几何图形和一些字母、数字及简单的文字组成，用来辨识货物，以防错发错运。运输标志通常由4个部分组成：（1）收货人或发货人的英文缩写字母或简称；（2）合同号；（3）目的港；（4）货物件数或件号。

指示性标志是一些醒目的简洁提示，以保证货物在搬运、储存和装卸过程中操作适当，如"小心轻放""此端向上"等，一般用黑色标注。

警告性标志由文字和特定的图案组成，又称危险货物包装标志。它是指在运输包装内装有爆炸品、易燃物品、有毒物品和放射性物质等危险货物时，必须在运输包装上标明用于各种危险品的标志，以示警告和保护物质与人身的安全，如"爆炸品""有毒品""有害品"等。

2. 与装运相关的外贸知识

装运是国际货物买卖合同中不可缺少的一项条款。装运条款（terms of shipment）一般包括运输方式、装运时间、装运及卸货港、分批装运和转船等。与装运相关的函电主要有：催装函、装船指示和装船通知等，这些函电多发生在订单确认和签约后的履约阶段。就交易磋商阶段而言，关于装运的信函并不多见。

国际贸易中，选择正确的运输方式很重要。运输方式包括海洋运输、铁路运输、航空运输、集装箱运输、国际多式联运、邮包运输、公路或内陆运输等。运输方式的选择具体取决于商品的特性、运输距离、交通工具情况、运输期限及运费等。但是，最常用也是最基本的国际贸易运输方式是海上货物运输。

根据运输方式的不同，海洋运输分为班轮运输和租船运输。班轮运输是指船舶按照固定的航线、固定的停靠港口、固定的船期表和相对固定的运费率开展运输。租船是指托运人与船东签订租船合同，租赁货船装运货物。如果出口货物数量较大，需要整船载运的，应办理租船手续；对出口货物数量不大，不需整船装运的，则应安排租订班轮或租订部分舱位运输。

装运时间是指将货物装上运输工具的时间或期限。在按 FOB、CFR 和 CIF 条件成交的情况下，卖方的装运时间以承运人在提单上签署的时间为依据。通常装运时间不是一个确切的时间，而是规定一个时间段，如"在收到相关信用证后30天内装运"。

装运港指的是发货的港口，卸货港则是目的港。在选择装运港和目的港时，货物所在位置、进口商、港口条件等应当被考虑进去。通常，出口商指定装运港，进口商指定目的港。

分批装运指的是同一合同项下多于一次的装运。这种情况往往涉及大宗出口，或者基于供货量限制和买方的特殊要求等。有时到达目的港的船只没有或稀少，这时候就不得不采用转船的方式。分批和转船都要经过买卖双方的协商，不能擅自由单方决定。

3. 保险相关外贸知识

保险与外贸业务紧密相连。国际贸易中的货物在长途运输中，包括装卸和存贮都可能会遇到难以预料的风险，从而导致货物发生损失。为消除贸易商对运输风险的后顾之忧，在货物装运前，结合不同的价格术语，卖方或买方通常向保险公司为货物投保，以转嫁或规避风险及损失。

保险条款是国际货物买卖合同的重要组成部分之一，一般包括投保险别、保险金额、保险费和保险单等。外贸业务中与保险相关的函电主要涉及提高保险金额、请求代办保险等，多由买方撰写，且经常是发生在签约后。

国际货物运输保险的种类包括海上、陆上、航空货物运输保险和邮包运输保险，其中以海上货物运输保险历史最久。中国人民保险公司（PICC）制定的"中国保险条款"（CIC），将海运货物保险险别分为基本险和附加险两类。基本险按照承包范围由小到大,被分为:平安险(FPA)、水渍险(WPA)和一切险(All Risks)3种。附加险包括11种一般附加险和8种特殊附加险,附加险不能单独投保。一切险除了包括平安险和水渍险的各项责任外,还包括11种一般附加险。

英国伦敦保险协会制定的《协会货物条款》(ICC)是国际上应用最为广泛的保险条款。它将保险险别分为6种:ICC(A)、ICC(B)、ICC(C)、协会货物战争险、协会货物罢工险、恶意损害险。除恶意损害险外,其他都可单独投保。

外贸业务中,保险金额一般是按货物CIF价格加成10%来计算,也就是发票金额的110%。保险费是保险金额与保险费率相乘的结果,不同险别费率不同。常用的保险单证主要有保险单和保险凭证。保险凭证是一种简化保险单,与保单具有同样的效力。

4. 支付相关外贸知识

商业活动的目的是盈利,如果付款不能得到保证,那么商业和贸易活动就失去了意义。因此,支付是国际贸易中非常重要的一环。支付相关信函通常包括:介绍和沟通付款方式、协商付款时间,以及与信用证操作相关的催证和改证函等。这些信函可由买方或卖方撰写,结合具体内容,在订单前后都有出现。

国际贸易中,常用的支付方式有3种:汇付、托收和信用证。

汇付是最简单的国际货款结算方式。采用汇付方式结算货款时,出口方将货物交付给进口方,由进口方径自通过银行将货款汇给出口方。汇付方式有3种:电汇(T/T)、信汇(M/T)和票汇(D/D),其中以电汇最为常用。汇付是以商业信用为基础的支付方式,实际业务中,根据付款时间不同有前T/T和后T/T,分别表现为先款后货和先货后款。这两种不同付款时间的电汇,对买卖双方的风险差异巨大。而对于大额订单的付款安排,用电汇方式更是难以解决。

托收是出口方委托银行向进口方收款的一种支付方式。托收有光票托收和跟单托收。光票托收是指出口方仅将金融票据(汇票)委托银行代为收款,一般多用于预付款或尾款支付。跟单托收是出口方发运货物后开立汇票连同货运单据,委托出口地银行通过其在进口地的分行或代理行向进口方收取货款。在具体业务中,依据银行对进口商的交单条件,跟单托收又分为付款交单(D/P, documents against payment)和承兑交单(D/A, documents against acceptance),付款交单又可分为即期付款交单(D/P at sight)和远期付款交单(D/P after sight)。对出口商而言,承兑交单的收汇风险远大于付款交单。

信用证是国际贸易中最常用的支付方式,它是银行承诺有条件付款的书面文件,是一种银行信用。进口商向银行(开证行)申请开立以出口人为受益人的信用证,开证行开出信用证并传递给出口方所在地的通知行,通知行核实后转交信用证给出口方。出口方装运后,缮制符合信用证要求的单据,银行审核单据无误后付款。信用证对于出口方而言,具有较大的收款安全性和保障性,尤其对于大额订单或者交易双方初次合作,都是较为合理的首选支付手段。

5.1.2 信函结构

交易细节沟通函电的正文内容结构一般包括3项。

（1）明确主题。对之前的信函表示感谢并告知对方此次写信的目的（清晰地表明这封邮件是关于某项或某些交易细节问题的告知和洽商）。

（2）陈述事实或说明具体要求。

（3）表示希望对方能够接受己方要求并予以关注，盼早日回复等。

回复对方交易细节沟通函电的正文内容结构一般也包括3项。

（1）感谢对方来函并告知此回信的目的（关于对方来函中某项或某些问题的回复）。

（2）确认对方要求或提出己方的不同意见和解决办法。

（3）表示希望对方能够认可以上意见和办法，盼早日回复等。

交易细节沟通信函涉及的主题和内容较多且杂乱，写作模板难以统一，以上信函结构仅供参考。撰写和回复这类信函的时间，一般在订单前后。可能是基于这些细节的磋商后才进入下订单和确认环节，也可能是在收到客户的订单后，要对相关的交易细节加以确认，以便开始生产。

5.2 Task and Project 任务和项目

Task 1: 阅读买方关于包装的信函并撰写回复函

☞ **业务背景和任务**

宁波J&R公司在报价并寄送样品后，于8月6日收到客户的邮件，内容如下：

例5-1: 买方关于包装要求的信函

Subject: Battery-Driver Toy Cars

Dear Monica,

We are satisfied with your samples and intend to place an order with you. We are now writing to you in regard to the packing of the captioned goods.

We suggest they should be wrapped in polythene wrappers and packed in cardboard boxes padded with foam plastic, ten toy cars each, 50 boxes to a wooden case lined with oil-cloth. We believe such packing will reduce any possible damage in transit to a minimum.

We trust that you will give careful consideration to our proposal.

Regards,

Mike

Notes

1. battery-driver：电动的

2. captioned goods：标题项下之货物

3. polythene wrapper：聚乙烯袋

4. padded with foam plastic：垫以塑料泡沫

5. a wooded case：木箱

6. lined with oil-cloth：内衬油布

7. …reduce any possible damage in transit to a minimum：将运输过程中可能的损失降到最低

8. proposal：建议，提议

☞ 阅读与写作任务

请仔细阅读客户关于包装要求的邮件（例5-1），并以宁波 J & R 公司业务员的身份，结合下列相关信息撰写回复函。

相关信息：宁波 J & R 公司从事各类电动玩具出口多年，一直以改良纸箱作为外包装包装货品出口。在纸箱内衬聚乙烯布，外以塑料包装带捆扎，完全能够保护货物在运输途中不因潮湿或颠簸和碰撞而受损。这种改良的纸箱包装适合长距离海运，已被客户广为接受和认可。

主管让你回复客户，向客户详细解释公司的惯常包装。同时，也要说明：如果客户坚持以木箱装运，我们也可以接受并且照做，毕竟客户至上是我们的宗旨。但是，额外的费用需由客户承担。

例 5-2：卖方回复并提出其他包装建议

Subject: Packing of Battery-Driver Toy Cars

Dear Mike,

Thank you for your email of August 6, confirming our samples together with your proposal of the packing of battery-driver toy cars.

As regards the packing, we could use wooden cases for the outer packing if you think better. We always have our clients' interest in mind. But, our improved packing with cartons for toy cars has been widely accepted by our regular clients. Up to now, there has not been a single complaint from any of them since our adoption of this packing. Our cartons are lined with polythene sheet, reinforced by overall strapping with plastic straps to protect the contents from moisture or any possible damage from jolting and collision in transit. Therefore, it is suitable for long distance ocean transportation.

Furthermore, by using carton, the packing cost and cargo weight can be reduced and freightage can be saved accordingly. If you insist on wooden cases for outer packing, we would strictly follow your instruction. Only that the extra charges should be borne by you.

We state the above for your reference and are awaiting your further comments.

Regards,

Monica

Notes

1. outer packing：外包装

2. have our clients' interest in mind：把客户的利益放在心上

3. adoption：采用

4. polythene sheet：聚乙烯布

5. reinforced by overall strapping with plastic straps：以塑料包装袋捆好

6. moisture：潮湿

7. jolting and collision：颠簸和碰撞

8. ocean transportation：海运

9. freightage：运费

10. the extra charges should be borne by you：额外的费用应由贵方承担

这两封关于包装的信函发生在订单确认和签约前，是买卖双方就合同条款中的包装问题进行沟通，以便能够顺利达成交易。

例5-1是买方提出包装要求的信函。全文三段，共五句，篇幅适中。第一段两句话，买方先表示了采购意愿，然后才点明主题，提出包装事宜。第二段是主体部分，具体陈述货物的包装要求和方法：从包装方式到包装材料都进行了详细说明。第三段是结尾段，希望卖方认真考虑并及时回应。

例5-2是卖方针对例5-1的来函的回复。全文四段，共十一句，篇幅相对较长。第一段用一句话感谢对方来函。第二段有六句话，是主体部分。首先就买方的包装要求给予肯定答复，接着用转折词引导来介绍自己的包装方式，并以其他客户的认可来消除买方对货物包装可能存在的疑虑，同时就包装细节也加以详尽地解释。第三段对买方包装要求引发的相关费用问题做了说明。第四段是结尾段，仍将决定权交予买方。

包装环节相关信函，可以是买方向卖方发出的，对于出口货物的包装提出具体的要求，希望卖方确认并遵照执行。也可以是卖方向买方发出的，就出口货物的包装问题及相关费用，提出建议或者解决方案，供买方认可或者提请双方讨论。

Task 2：阅读买方关于支付的信函并撰写回复函

☞ **业务背景和任务**

经过前段时间的沟通，宁波 J & R 公司于 8 月 10 日收到客户的邮件，内容如下：

例5-3：买方关于支付条款的信函

Subject: Stainless-Steel Cutlery

Dear Monica,

We are the largest department store in Kuwait and have recently received a number of enquiries for your stainless-steel cutlery. We think there are good prospects for the sale of this cutlery, but at present it is little known here and as we can not count on regular sales, we do not feel able to make purchases on our own account.

We are therefore writing to suggest that you send us a trial delivery for sale on D/A terms. We make the proposal, hoping to place firm orders when the market is established.

We believe our proposal offers good prospects and hope you will be willing to accept.

Regards,

Mike

Notes

1. stainless-steel cutlery：不锈钢刀具

2. department store：百货公司

3. prospect：前景

4. little known：了解甚少

5. count on：指望；依靠

6. regular sales：常规销售；定期销售

7. on our own account：为自己的利益；自负盈亏

8. D/A documents against acceptance：承兑交单

9. firm orders：稳定的订单

☞ **阅读与写作任务**

请仔细阅读客户关于支付方式的邮件（例5-3），并以宁波 J & R 公司业务员的身份，结合下列相关信息撰写回复函。

主管让你回复客户，向客户解释信用证付款是公司的惯例，尤其对于新客户，目前恐怕不能接受承兑交单的付款方式，希望对方可以理解。

例5-4：卖方回复买方关于支付条款的信函

Subject: Stainless-Steel Cutlery

Dear Mike,

Thank you for your letter of August 10th on our stainless-steel cutlery.

As regards your proposal for D/A terms, we wish to point out that payment by L/C is our usual practice, and we are afraid we are not in a position to accept it as an exceptional case.

I regret to say that we must adhere to our usual practice and sincerely hope that this will not affect our business relations.

Best regards,

Monica

Notes

1. proposal：建议
2. usual practice：惯例
3. adhere：坚持

这两封关于支付的信函发生在订单确认前，是买卖双方就合同条款中的支付问题进行沟通，以便能够顺利达成交易。

例5-3是买方就支付方式提出建议的信函。全文三段，共五句，篇幅适中。第一段两句话，其中第二句较长。买方先表示当地存在需求，产品有销售前景，接着解释了采购意愿，并为支付方式的提出做了铺垫。第二段提出建议的支付方式，并做了一定的说服。第三段再次跟进，希望卖方认真考虑。

例5-4是卖方针对例5-3的来函的回复。全文三段，共三句，篇幅相对短一些。第一段用一句话感谢对方来函。第二段是主体，直接告知对方不能接受提出的支付条款，并做了简要解释。第三段是结尾段，再次重申己方关于支付方式的立场。

支付环节相关信函，可以是买方就支付方式提出具体的建议和要求，希望卖方接受并遵照执行。也可以是卖方向买方介绍常用的支付方式，以供买方选择或提请双方协商。还可以是卖方针对买方提出的某种具体支付方式，回函接受并详述操作细节或者回函拒绝并解释原因。

5.3 Actual Case Letters 实战信函

国际贸易业务中,在价格确定之后,买卖双方的其他交易细节沟通会从订单确认之前,一直持续到合同签署之后,沟通内容也是包罗万象。不仅有上述提到的包装、支付和装运等交易环节,还有样品问题、颜色沟通、确认设计稿等方方面面的细节。而实际业务中,由于英文水平和撰写人的写作习惯不同,以及具体业务和主题差异等原因,这类信函的篇幅、内容和结构具有多样性和复杂性。

以下多封实战案例,供学习者借鉴和参考。

例5-5: 卖方关于包装的沟通信

Subject: Packing Issues

Dear Mike,

As per your order, the packing is poly bag with printing, right?

But our previous discussion is just poly bag, with no any other additional charge. If you insist on the printing on poly bag, we have to increase the unit price a little.

By the way, we could do a sticker for you, and put the right side on each poly bag, free of charge.

Please advise your decision. Thanks.

Regards,

Monica

Notes
1. poly bag: 塑料袋
2. sticker: 标签
3. free of charge: 免费

这封函电发生在订单确认前。这是卖方在收到买方的订单后,针对订单中关于包装的问题,提出的不同意见,同时也给出了解决方案,以便双方能就包装问题达成一致。

邮件正文篇幅是四段,共五句话。第一段以问句开头,明确主题。第二段用两句话,指出订单中包装条款存在的矛盾,以及会引发的费用问题。第三段用一句话给出了我方的建议和免费解决方案。然后就是一句话的结尾段。

这封卖方撰写的商讨包装问题的实战案例信函，为买卖双方就交易细节产生分歧和不同意见时，提供了一个解决方案和撰写回复的思路。首先是明确双方的分歧点，接着指出这个矛盾将会引发的后续费用或其他问题，然后跟进提出合理可行的解决方案，以更好地促进交易达成。

例5-6：卖方关于支付的沟通信

Subject: Payment for 6 Pcs Screwdriver Set

Dear Mike,

As regards 6 pcs screwdriver set, we could confirm the price and quantity for this order.

But we cannot accept T/T 30 days. If you insist on doing T/T instead of L/C, we will ONLY use T/T after copy of B/L.

Please advise your decision. Thanks

Regards,

Monica

Notes

1. 6 pcs screwdriver set：螺丝刀6件套
2. T/T after copy of B/L：凭提单副本付款

　　这封函电发生在订单确认前。这实际上是一封关于支付条款的还盘信，结构清晰且词句简洁。首先，第一段并没有按常规直奔主题，而是先确认双方已经达成共识的交易内容。第二段是核心段，用了转折词but做开头，表意非常清晰。先是概括了双方的分歧，接着提出了我方的折中性解决方案。第三段是简洁地跟进性督促回复。

　　在国际贸易中，支付是非常重要的交易磋商环节。很多情况下，支付方式的选择和确认是决定这笔生意能否进行或者顺利进行下去的关键。有些时候，客户指定的付款方式和我们要求的收款方式是有巨大差异的。卖方希望能在发货前收进所有货款，这样就能最大程度地避免损失和潜在风险。反过来，买方最希望的则是先收货后付款。这种情况下，就需要通过进一步沟通来找到双方共同能够接受的方式。

例5-7：进口商来函商议保险事宜

Subject: S/C No. 202

Dear Monica,

We wish to refer you to the 500 cases electronic toys under S/C No. 202, from which we have noticed that the goods are to be covered against A.R. for 110% of the invoice value.

As your offer is on CIF basis, the shipment should be insured at your end according to the contract. In order to make the goods safer and prevent pilferage in transportation, we shall be pleased if you will arrange to insure the goods on our behalf against all risks and additional T. P. N. D. at 130% of the invoice value.

We sincerely hope that our request will meet with your approval.

Best regards,

Mike

Notes

1. refer you to：请你参看……

2. cover against：投保……（险别）

3. A. R = All Risks：一切险

4. insure：保险；投保

5. at your end：在你方

6. pilferage：偷盗，行窃

7. on our behalf：代表我方

8. T. P. N. D：偷窃、提货不着险（一种特殊附加险）

9. meet with your approval：得到你的同意

　　这封函电发生在签约后。这是一封买方撰写的，要求卖方提高保险金额，并增加保险险别的商议保险事宜的信函。在原合同中已经确认的保险险别为一切险，保险金额为发票价值的110%。而买方在这个邮件中提出加保一个特殊附加险：偷窃、提货不着险，同时要求将保险金额提高至发票价值的130%。

　　国际贸易中，在货物运输之前，需要为货物办理保险事宜。不同价格术语下，办理投保和支付保费的对象是不同的。一般来说，CIF条件下是由卖方负责办理保险并支付保费。FOB和CFR条件下，则是买方负责办理保险并支付保费。

对于买方关于更改保险事宜的此类相关要求，卖方在能够做到的前提下，应尽量予以满足。但同时要注意应及时跟买方沟通因增加险种和提升保额而导致的额外费用问题，按惯例应由买方承担相关额外费用。

例5-8：讨论颜色问题

Subject: Color Approval

Dear Mike,

Thank you for your kind notice. Please hereby re-confirm the color for your orders.

PWX 192 （orange）, 2,500 pcs

PWX 183 （green）, 1,500 pcs

PWX 174 （light blue）, 1,000 pcs

If no problem, we'll send you some color pieces before mass production for approval.

Regards,

Monica

Notes

1. color pieces：色块

2. mass production：大货生产

视频5.2

产品的颜色问题有时也是交易细节沟通的内容之一，这封实战信函就是卖方要求买方确认产品颜色相关事项的交易细节沟通信。这种信函一般在订单确认前后，但一定在订单操作和正式生产之前。

商品的颜色是重要的问题。有些产品在订单环节很容易遇到颜色纠纷，如纺织品类、部分轻工类等。因为提供的颜色跟客户的要求发生偏差，从而导致严重的色差，而这种情况是大部分客户无法接受的，往往会直接造成客户的退货或者索赔。在实际工作中，如果是客户指定颜色，那么在订单最终确认或者大货生产前，必须跟客户确认好产品的颜色和对应的色卡号，然后根据色号提供产前样或色块给客户做最终确认，确认以后才能正式安排生产。

例5-9：确认设计稿

Subject: Artwork Confirming

Dear Mike,

Please find the files attachment, with details below:

1. Artwork for shipping mark
2. Artwork for PDQ
3. Draft for multi-language warning on poly bag.

Kindly check and give us final approval ASAP.

If any problems, pls let me know. We'll revise them soon.

Regards,

Monica

Notes

1. artwork：设计稿
2. PDQ：展示盒
3. multi-language：多国语言

　　这封实战信函是关于交易细节沟通的另一项内容：确认设计稿。在这封邮件里，卖方列出并以附件形式明确了3个项目的设计稿，要求买方尽快确认。

　　在签约前或者正式生产前，产品内外包装相关的设计稿也是需要一并确认的，如唛头、展示盒包装、多国语言说明书、商标、条形码的设计稿等等。这些细节都需要罗列清楚且一一对应，一旦事后发生问题再补救，不仅会耽误双方的时间，同时也会在经济上造成损失。

　　这两个关于交易细节的沟通信函，可能不是每笔外贸业务中都一定会涉及的，但同时也是最容易被忽略的。这类交易细节沟通信函，整体上写作难度不大，表意上具有简洁化、清晰化和具体化的特征。在外贸业务中，多由卖方撰写，并要求客户明确地回复或确认。

5.4 Summary小结

　　本章将进出口合同条款中除价格以外的交易条款做了一个汇总梳理，并结合外贸业务实践增加了其他内容，合并为交易细节沟通专题。整章以出口业务为主导，突出实战，强化写作能力训练和商务思维养成，展示并分析了9封交易细节沟通信函，覆盖面广且实用性强。

这类函电，结合不同的内容，撰写和回复时间可能会在订单确认前后或者订单执行期间。有时，也会将几项交易条件合并到一封邮件中汇总陈述和说明。

写作注意事项：

1. 包装相关信函

包装相关主题主要涉及包装方式、包装材料、唛头和包装费用等。具体内容可以是：买方向卖方提出包装要求的信函，卖方主动向买方介绍包装情况的信函，或者是双方互相回复的信函等。

在书写或回复这类信函时，出口方可以向进口方详细描述其习惯包装方式，同时也可说明可以接受进口方的包装要求，但额外费用应由进口方承担。如果要更改有关包装的任何条款，都必须在装运前经双方商讨同意后确定。

2. 装运相关信函

在外贸业务中，装运相关的往来函电主要有：卖方发出的装运通知、买方发出的装运指示函和催装函，以及因情况突然变化而产生的双方商议修改原装运条件的函电等。

装船通知是在货物装船后，卖方发给买方关于货物已装运的详细信息，以便买方做好接货和付款的准备。

装运指示函，一般是基于F组价格条款，如以FOB和FCA等价格术语成交的情况。货物的装运由买方负责，买方租船订舱后要及时通知卖方关于船名、航次、装船地点和预计的装运时间等信息，以便双方做好船货衔接。

催装函是买方未能及时收到任何有关装运方面的消息，因而催促卖方尽快安排装运，以免延误交货的信函。信函内容一般包括3项：首先是陈述未收到装运信息的事实，其次是说明应及时装运的理由，如满足市场急需或销售季等，然后就是对迅速办理装运事宜的督促。

在实际业务中，这类函电多发生在订单执行和履约环节，因此将在后续章节进一步学习。

3. 保险相关信函

外贸业务中保险相关的往来函电包括：买方要求提高保险金额、买方请求卖方代办保险、卖方的回复函、买方或卖方写给保险公司的信函等。

在书写保险类信函时，应做到简洁、清晰和明了。如果是提出某种请求的一方，应明确告知对方自己的要求，不要让对方产生歧义。而回复信函的一方，应做到及时和礼貌周到，要清楚地表明是否能够满足对方要求，并对产生的相应费用进行明确，同时也可提出其他的合理性建议。

4. 支付相关信函

支付是国际贸易中非常重要且复杂的环节。买卖双方支付相关往来函电主要有：卖方建议支付方式的信函、买方提出更改支付方式的信函、出口商拒绝或同意对方更改付款方式的信函、双方协商付款时间的信函，以及与信用证操作相关的催证、审证和改证函等。

撰写支付相关信函,要注意词句得体,表意准确。涉及更改支付条款或者拒绝对方提议的信函,应注意给出原因和说明理由。同时,要将自己的意见和观点明确地表述清楚,避免纠纷和歧义。业务沟通中,要注意体谅对方,但同时也要态度坚决,不可轻易地退让。

价格是交易磋商的核心,但是价格以外的其他交易条款,对于交易能否达成和顺利进行,也是极为重要的。特别是对于新客户而言,这些交易细节都要逐一沟通清楚并加以确认,以免引发后续纠纷。

在国际贸易中,结合不同的业务背景、贸易关系和沟通内容,这类函电发送和回复的时间并不统一。双方可能是在下订单前就加以明确相关交易细节,以便确认订单和签约;也可能是在订单确认后,双方就某项条款进一步补充说明和调整,以便顺利地执行订单。

5.5 Useful Words & Expressions 实用词汇及短语

1. pack

v. 打包;包装

repack

v. 重新包装;改装

We have packed the goods under Order No. H223 in wooden case. 我们已将第H223号订单项下的货物用木箱包装。

It is our usual way to pack these goods in cartons. 我们通常采用纸箱包装。

pack off 包装发往;寄出

We have packed the samples off to you. 我们已将样品寄给贵方。

pack away 把……装起来

All the chinaware was carefully packed away in cases and stored in the warehouse. 所有瓷器都被小心地包装起来,并储藏在仓库里。

常用的"包装方式"的表述有:

(1)in... 表示用某种容器包装

Walnuts are packed in double gunny bags. 核桃用双层麻袋包装。

(2)in... of... each 表示用某种容器包装,每一容器内装若干

Men's shirts are packed in wooden case of 10 dozen each. 男士衬衫用木箱装,每箱10打。

(3) ...in... each containing... 用某种容器包装,每一容器内装若干

Nylon socks are packed in wooden case, each containing 50 dozen. 尼龙袜用木箱包装,每箱装50打。

(4) ...to... 表示将若干件装于某一容器内

Folding chairs are packed 2 pieces to a carton. 一个纸板箱装两把折叠椅。

(5)each... in... and... to... 表示先将每单位装入某种容器,再将若干单位装另一种较大的容器

Each pair of nylon socks is packed in a plastic bag and 12 pairs to a box. 每双尼龙袜装一

个塑料袋，12双装一盒。

（6）…to… and… to　表示先将若干单位装进某种容器，再把若干此种容器装入另一种较大的容器

Pens are packed 12 pieces to a box and 200 boxes to a wooden case. 12支钢笔装一盒，200盒装一个木箱。

packing

n. 包装；包装材料；包装方法；包装费

The packing must be seaworthy. 该包装必须适合海运。

We need a lot of packing to protect these glasses. 我们需要大量的包装材料以保护这些玻璃器皿。

We offer these shirts at USD20 each, plus postage and packing. 这些衬衫我方报价为每件20美元，外加邮资和包装费。

与包装相关的短语：

inner packing 内包装

outer packing 外包装

neutral packing 中性包装

customary packing 习惯包装

export packing 出口包装

packing list　装箱单

packing instructions　包装要求；包装须知

packing method　包装方式

packing charges 包装费用

package

n. 中小型的包裹（指包、捆、束、箱等）；"一揽子"交易

Each package should be marked "Fragile". 每件包装上都要标明"易碎品"。

The computer is sold with a printer and software as part of the package. 这台计算机与打印机和软件一并销售。

packet

*n.*小包（= a small package）;（计算机）数据包，信息包

The packets of tea are intact. 该批茶叶的包装完好无损。

部分常用的出口包装容器如下。

case（箱）: wooden case（木箱）; iron case（铁箱）; crate（板条箱）; carton（纸箱）。

drum（桶）: wooden drum（木桶）; iron drum（铁桶）; plastic drum（塑料桶）。

bag（袋）: cloth bag（布袋）; gunny bag（麻袋）; paper bag（纸袋）; plastic bag（塑料袋）。

bottle（瓶）: cylinder（钢瓶）; flask（长颈瓶）; jar（坛）; box（盒）。

basket（篓）; pallet（托盘）; bale（捆包）; container（集装箱）。

2. container

n. 集装箱

相关词汇及短语有：

dry cargo container 干货集装箱

refrigerator container 冷藏集装箱

open top container 开顶集装箱

tank container 罐式集装箱

flat rack container 框架集装箱

dress hanger container 挂衣集装箱

FCL: full container load 整装

LCL: less than container load 拼装

CY：container yard 集装箱堆场（整柜出运）

CFS: container freight station 集装箱货运站

Please ship the goods by CY. 请安排整柜装运。

I could accept the CFS delivery. 我可以接受散货。

3. lined with 以……作为内衬

相关表述：

lined with oil-cloth 内衬油布

lined with kraft paper 内衬牛皮纸

lined with fresco bag 内衬锡箔袋

lined with moist proof paper 内衬防潮纸

lined with thin paper 包内衬薄纸

lined with aluminum foil in the wooden case 木箱内衬铝箔纸

4. have our clients' interest in mind 把客户的利益放在心上

5. moisture

n. 潮湿

Those cartons are well protected against moisture by plastic lining. 由于箱内铺有塑料衬里，防潮性能良好。

The wheat you shipped per m. v. "Star" contains too much moisture. 你方由"星"号货轮运送来的小麦含水量太高。

6. ship

v. 装运；装上船

The goods will be shipped in one lot. 这些货物将一次装运。

n. 船

shipbuilding

n. 造船业

shipment

n. 装运；装运期限；到货

Please arrange shipment as soon as possible. 请尽快安排装运。

Please extend shipment 30 days. 请将装运期限延长30天。

Quality must be the same as your last shipment. 品质应与上次到货一致。

装运相关短语：

mode of shipment　运输方式

time of shipment　装运时间

port of shipment　装运港

partial shipment　分批装运

transshipment　转船；转运

shipping

n. 船舶；船舶总吨位数；航运；装运；运输

The shipping space for sailing to London up to the end of this month has been fully booked up. 本月底驶往伦敦的舱位已订满。

Their shipping exceeds that of any other country. 他们的船舶总吨位超过任何其他国家。

相关短语：

shipping service　航运业

shipping mark　装船标志；装运唛头

shipping advice 装运通知

shipping order　装货单；下货纸

shipping space 舱位

shipping instruction　装运须知；装船指示（买方发给卖方关于装运的要求和注意事项）

We await your shipping instruction. 我们等待贵方装运须知。

shipping documents 装运单据

一套装运单据（one set of shipping documents），主要包括以下8种。

（1）Bill of Lading（B/L）提单

（2）Commercial Invoice　发票

（3）Certificate of Quality 质量证明书

（4）Certificate of Quantity 数量证明书

（5）Certificate of Origin（C/O）产地证

（6）Insurance Policy 保险单

（7）Weigh Memo 重量单

（8）Packing List 装箱单

装运当事人：

shipper　发货人；托运人；货主

consignor　发货人

consignee 收货人

carrier 承运人

forwarder 货运代理人

7. freight

n. 运费；货物（特指装载于车船、飞机上的）

相关短语：

freight charges 运费

freight agency 运货代理商

freight forwarder 运输公司

freight rate 运费率

freight service 货运

freight tariff 运费表

freightage 运费

freight prepaid 运费预付

freight paid 运费已付

freight collect 运费到付

freight payable at destination 运费到付

8. bill of lading 提单

提单常缩写为B/L。

9. All Risks 一切险

一切险可缩写为A. R；一切险是中国人民保险公司（PICC）制定的中国保险条款（China Insurance Clauses, 缩略形式为CIC或C.I.C.）中的海洋运输货物保险条款所包含的3个基本险别之一。其他两个基本险别是平安险和水渍险。

平安险：Free from Particular Average, 缩写为F.P.A. 或FPA。

水渍险：With Particular Average, 缩写为W.P.A 或WPA。

除以上3个基本险外，还有附加险（extraneous risks），包括一般附加险、特殊附加险和特别附加险。

一般附加险有11种，如下所示。

偷窃提货不着险：Theft, Pilferage and Non-Delivery Risks（简称T. P. N. D. 或TPND）

短量险：Shortage Risk or Risk of Shortage

混杂、玷污险：Intermixture and Contamination Risks

渗漏险：Leakage Risks or Risk of Leakage

碰损、破碎险：Clash and Breakage Risks

钩损险：Hook Damage Risk

锈损险：Rust Risk or Risk of Rust

包装破裂险：Breaking of Packing Risk

受潮受热险：Sweating and Heating Risks

串味险：Taint of Odor Risks

常见的特殊附加险有2种，分别为战争险和罢工、暴动、民变险。

战争险：War Risk

罢工、暴动、民变险：Strikes，Riots and Civil Commotions（缩写为S. R. C. C.或SRCC）；这个险别没有risks这个词

常见的特别附加险有6种，如下所示。

交货不到险：Failure to Delivery Risk

进口关税险：Import Duty Risk

舱面险：On Deck Risk

拒收险：Rejection Risk

黄曲霉素险：Aflatoxin Risk

出口到港、澳地区（包括九龙）的货物存仓火险：Fire Risk Extension Clause for Storage of Cargo at Destination Hong Kong（including Kowloon）or Macao

在函电中说各个险别时，除All Risks 和 War Risk 外，risk(s) 这个词通常略去，如：

We shall cover WPA and TPND on your order. 我们将对贵方订单投保水渍险和偷窃、提货不着险。

The goods are to be insured against leakage. 此货需保渗漏险。

10. insure

v. 保险；投保

Please insure against Shortage Risk. 请投保短量险。

Please insure the goods against All Risks and War Risk. 请将此批货物投保一切险和战争险。

insurance

n. 保险

I would like to have the insurance of the goods covered at 110% of the invoice value. 我们希望货物能够按照发票金额的110%投保。

在表示"投保""办理保险"时，常与insurance搭配的动词有to arrange/cover/effect insurance。

We have covered insurance on the 100 metric tons of wool for 110% of the invoice value against all risks. 我方已将100吨羊毛按照发票金额的110%投保一切险。

insurance on＋所投保的货物，如 insurance on the 100 tons of wool。

insurance against＋投保的险别，如 insurance against FPA。

insurance with＋所投保的保险公司，如 insurance with the People's Insurance Company of China。

insurance at＋保险费或保险费率，如 insurance at the rate of 5%。

insurance　company　保险公司

insurance　agent　保险代理人

insurance　certificate　保险凭证

insurance coverage 保险范围

insurance amount 保险金额

insurer

n. 保险公司；保险人；保险业者

11. coverage

n. 保险范围；投保金额；保证金

He has fire and theft coverage on his store. 他给自己的商店投保了火险和盗窃险。

Regarding insurance, the coverage is for 110% of the invoice value up to the port of destination. 关于保险，按发票金额的110%投保，至目的港为止。

12. premium

n. 保险费

13. insurance policy 保险单

insurance certificate 保险凭证

14. the captioned goods 标题项下之货物

类似的表述还有：the subject goods, the article mentioned in the subject line。

15. the extra charges should be borne by you 额外的费用应由贵方承担

16. department store 百货公司；百货商店

17. account

n. & *v.* 账目；账户；理由；报账；认为

Our bank does not keep an RMB account with the Bank of China, Head Office, Beijing. 我方银行没有在北京的中国银行总行开立人民币账户。

These expenses of different kinds should be separately accounted for. 这些不同种类的支出应分别列账。

on account 作为部分账款；以赊账方式

on account of 由于……

on one's own account 自己承担风险

He owed USD 200 and sent me USD 50 on account. 他欠200美元，先给我50美元作为部分偿还。

We both understand our slippers are very popular in your market on account of their superior quality and competitive price. 我们双方都知道我方拖鞋因价廉物美而畅销于贵方市场。

They do not feel able to make purchase on their own account. 他们不能自负盈亏来购进货物。

18. D/A

D/A=documents against acceptance 承兑交单

19. D/P

D/P =documents against payment 付款交单

20. refer

v. 参照；提交；接洽

We refer you to our letter of June 6th. 请贵方参阅我方6月6日函。

We have referred them to you for their requirements. 我们已请他们就相关要求与贵方进行接洽。

refer to 谈及；提交

We refer to our letter of March 15th. 兹谈及我方3月15日函。

Your enquiry for bicycles has been referred to our sister corporation for attention. 贵方有关自行车的询价已交由我兄弟公司办理。

refer to sb. for sth. 向某人查询某事

Please refer to the Bank of China, Ningbo Branch for our credit standing. 请向中国银行宁波分行查询我方资信情况。

reference

n. 参阅；关于；参考；证人

Please make reference to our cable of June 4th. 请参阅我方6月4日电报。

With reference to your letter of May 6th, we will take the matter into serious consideration. 关于贵方5月6日来函，我方将认真考虑此事。

for your reference 供……参考

For your reference, we enclose a copy of our latest catalogue. 随函附寄我方最新目录一份，供贵方参考。

21. on our behalf 代表我们，代表我方

They are nominated to inspect the goods on our behalf. 他们被指派代表我们去验货。

22. meet with your approval 得到你的同意

We hope the term of payment will meet with your approval. 我们希望这个支付方式能得到你方同意。

23. mass production 大货生产；大规模生产；大量生产

24. artwork

n. 插图；插画；艺术作品

artwork design 原图设计；设计稿

25. PDQ 展示盒

Our products include color box, PDQ, corrugated box and poster. 我们的产品包括彩盒、展示盒、瓦楞纸箱和海报。

26. multi-language 多国语言；多语种；多语言

5.6 Useful Sentences 实用语句

1. Each pair of nylon socks is packed in a plastic bag and 12 pairs to a box.

每双尼龙袜装一个塑料袋，12双装一盒。

2. The dimensions of the carton are 18 cm high, 30 cm wide and 50 cm long with a volume of about 0.026 cubic meter.

该纸板箱尺码是高18厘米，宽30厘米，长50厘米，容积约为0.026立方米。

3. Our export trip scissors are packed in boxes of one dozen each, 100 boxes to a carton.

我方出口的旅行剪刀每盒装一打，每一纸板箱装一百盒。

4. Since a polythene bag is used for each underwear, it is all ready for window display and looks attractive.

因每件衬衣都用塑料袋进行了包装，所以适合橱窗陈列，并且看上去吸引人注意。

5. Please mark the bags according to the drawing given.

请按照所给的图样在袋上刷唛头。

6. We must make it clear that with the different packing materials the packing expenses will be different.

我们必须说清楚，采用不同的包装材料，包装费会不一样。

7. Each bicycle is enclosed in a corrugated cardboard pack, and 5 are banded together and wrapped in sheet plastic.

每辆自行车用瓦楞硬纸板箱包装，每5件捆扎在一起，并用塑料薄膜包装。

8. We take pleasure in notifying you that the goods under S/C No. 225 have been dispatched by M/V "Taishan" sailing on August 28 to Hong Kong.

我方高兴地通知贵方第225号合同下的货物已由"泰山"号轮发运，货物已于8月28日开往香港。

9. Since there is no direct vessel, we have to arrange multimodal combined transport by rail and sea.

由于没有直达船只，我们只好安排海陆联运。

10. If you agree to have the goods in two equal lot, please let us know so that we can make agreements accordingly.

如果你方同意分成等量的两批货物装运，请告知我方以便照此安排装运事宜。

11. We have the pleasure to enclose the invoice amounting to USD100,000, together with the bill of lading, both of which will find in order.

随函寄去总额10万美元的发票及提单各一份，请查收。

12. We acknowledge receipt of your confirmation that your consignment should be sent by air-freight, and we have accordingly forwarded the goods.

兹确认收到贵方要求将货物空运的确认函，我方已按照指示发送了该批货物。

13. According to the terms in the contract, shipping the goods is to be made in two equal

monthly installments.

根据合同条款，这批货分两批等量装运，每月装运一次。

14. If the buyer requires additional risks to be covered, the extra premium is for the buyer's account.

如果买方要求附加险，额外的保险费由买方承担。

15. We usually effect insurance against All Risks for the invoice value plus 10% for the goods sold on CIF basis.

我们通常以CIF条件下发票金额加成10%来为货物办理一切险。

16. Our usual terms of payment are by a confirmed irrevocable L/C by draft at sight.

我们通常的支付方式是以保兑的不可撤销的凭即期汇票支付的信用证。

17. We shall refund to you the premium upon receiving your debt note or you may draw on us at sight for the amount required.

我们收到你方借项清单后返还保险费，或者你方按所付金额向我方开出即期汇票。

18. In order to conclude the business, I hope you will meet me half way. What about 50% by L/C and 50% by D/P?

为了做成这笔交易，希望双方各让一半。50%以信用证付款，另外50%按付款交单如何？

19. 30% will be paid for deposit by T/T before production arranged, the balance is to be paid before shipment.

30%定金在投入生产前通过电汇支付，余款在装运前支付。

20. We agree to accept the goods in 3 shipments and you may draw on us at 60 days from the date of dispatch of each shipment.

我们同意货物分3批装运，贵方可向我方开立自每笔货物运输日起的60天远期汇票。

5.7 Exercises 练习

I Translate the following words and expressions into English or Chinese.

1. 中性包装
2. 一切险
3. 集装箱
4. 托运人
5. 水渍险
6. B/L
7. D/P
8. PDQ
9. freight prepaid
10. insurance policy

📱 Key 5.1

II Choose the best answer.

1. We could do a sticker for you, and put the right side on each poly bag, free of _____ .

A. cost   B. packing   C. money   D. charge

2. If you insist on the printing on poly bag, we have to _____ the unit price a little.

A. adjust   B. decrease   C. develop   D. increase

3.On receipt of your remittance _____ US $20,000 as per the enclosed invoice we will release your order _____ the forwarders.

A. by; to   B. about; of   C. for; to   D. about; for

4. Pens are packed 12 pieces _____ a box and 200 boxes _____ a wooden case.

A. to, in   B. to, to   C. in, to   D. to, of

5. Would you like to ship them by LCL or _____ ?

A. FCL   B. B/L   C. L/C   D. CTN

6. We give you on the attached full details _____ packing and marking.

A. regarding   B. be regarded   C. regarded   D. regard

7. If shipment involves transport by more than two modes, a (n) _____ will been issued.

A. direct B/L   B. ocean through B/L C. multi-modal B/L   D. shipped B/L

8. We are in _____ need of these goods.

A. very   B. urgent   C. real   D. now

9. Please note that the insurance on our CIF terms _____ All Risks for 110% of the invoice value.

A. makes   B. takes   C. covers   D. ourselves to be

10. Please effect insurance _____ your side covering All Risks and War Risk.

A. on   B. for   C. to   D. with

III Translate the following sentences into English or Chinese.

1. 货物用木箱包装,每箱20打。

2. 条形码应该标在内包装上。

3. 请告知订单备妥待运估计所需的时间。

4. 我们已经为货物投保了一切险和战争险。

5. 通常我们接受即期信用证付款,从不接受货到付款的方式。

6. Each case is lined with foam plastics in order to protect the goods against press.

7. We usually pack each piece of men's shirt in a box, half dozen to a carton and 10 dozen to a wooden case.

8. Please advise us 30 days before the month of the shipment of the contract number, name of commodity, quantity, port of loading and time when the goods reach the port of loading.

9. I hope you would leave us some leeway in terms of payment.

10. On receipt of your remittance for USD 20,000 as per the enclosed invoice, we will

release your order to the forwarders.

IV Translate the following body of the letter into English.

我们收到贵方7月13日来函，信中要求我们将全部5,000公吨麦子一批装船发运。非常抱歉，我们不能照办。

在我们就这批货物报盘时，就已经明确规定九月份装运。如果你方要求提前装运，我们尽最大努力也只能是8月份装运3,000公吨，剩下的2,000公吨9月份发运。

希望我们的建议令贵公司满意。如果你方接受这样的安排，请尽早告知我方。

我们希望做出相应的安排，所以，如能尽早获悉贵方的确认，我们将不胜感激。

V Translate the following body of the letter into Chinese.

We write to inform you that the articles are requested to be wrapped in corrugated paper and packed in strong wooden cases with excelsior, which must be battened, nailed and secured with metal straps all over.

Please limit the weight of any cases to 100 kg, and mark all the cases with an A in the square. Overall measurements of each case must not exceed 5ft (H) ×3ft (W) ×3ft (D) .

Please minimize the packing expenses as we expect it to the expensive.

We look forward to your early confirmation and advising us the shipment date.

VI Writing task.

Write a letter as per the following background and information.

某公司6月8日收到客户（David Smith）来函，提出以60天承兑交单付款方式替代即期信用证。经过慎重考虑，公司同意通融付款条件，但是同意即期付款交单而不是客户提出的60天远期承兑交单。

主管让你给客户回函告知此事，说服客户接受此交易条件。可以告知客户随着交易发展将会采用更灵活的付款方式。目前货物已经备妥待运，收到客户对付款方式的确认后就可以如期安排装运了。同时也希望这次付款方式的通融带来更多的订单。

5.8 Supplement & Extension 补充与拓展

合适的付款方式

出口商从事贸易行业，自然需要跟钱打交道。出口商要付款给下游工厂或者采购原材料，要把生产完成的产品卖给客户，甚至还要垫付一部分或者全部的货代费用，因此，付款方式的安全性不容忽视。一个不小心就有可能赔了夫人又折兵，损失了钱财也搭上了货物，钱货两空无处申冤，绝对是不好受的。因此，供应商总是寄希望于付款方式的安全，情愿降低利润，都要控制住风险。钱可以慢慢赚，但一旦上当，那可能就连续几个月甚至几年都白干了。

那有没有绝对安全的付款方式呢？理论上是有的，就是100%前T/T，英文叫T/T in advance或者T/T 100% in advance。在生产前收进所有货款，自然是最安全的，钱在手则心不慌，至少不用担心客户不付钱，不用担心货物被轻易骗走。

这么一来，我们是安全了，那客户呢？他们就要承担所有的风险。生意是相互的，一方零风险，另一方就承担了百分之百的风险。客户会答应吗？也许会，但大多数情况下不会。只要他有别的选择，只要他能在别人那里找到替代品，他就不会答应。专业的买家或者大买家，不到万不得已是绝对不会接受前T/T这种付款方式的。那这样一来，就会通过具体的谈判来讨价还价，彼此让步，最终达成共识。

如果从出口商的角度，将几种常用的付款方式，根据风险的大小由小到大进行排列，则排序如下：

T/T 100% in advance（预付货款）< T/T with deposit, the rest balanced before shipment（部分定金，部分装船前付款）< L/C at sight（即期信用证）< L/C ×× days（远期信用证）< T/T 100% before shipment（装运前付款）< T/T with deposit, the rest balanced copy of B/L（部分定金，部分凭提单副本）< D/P（付款交单）< T/T by copy of B/L（见提单副本付款）< D/A（承兑交单）< T/T ×× days（后TT）< O/A（赊销）。

显然，全收钱最安全，全放账最不安全，至于中间具体选择哪个，则要看双方的协商和谈判水平。

一般来说，中小客户接受T/T的可能性比较大，不论有没有订金，这些都可以谈。但是大客户基本上都是以O/A和各种远期付款为主。这种情况需要一分为二来看。

如果是直接做大买家（direct to big customers），恐怕很难有谈判付款方式的可能。因为他们都有很多稳定的供应商，选择很多，买方实力远远高过卖方，本身在谈判上就不平等，对方很难自降身价来满足或迁就供应商来做T/T。除非价格特别有竞争力，以这些特殊的条件来换取买方在付款方式上的让步，则是有可能的。

如果是通过中间商来做大买家（indirect to big customer），那就容易很多。因为中间商存在的价值，就是大买家为了规避风险，或者是看中他们的分销能力、对各种资源和渠道的优势、出色的设计能力等而做出的理性选择。这样，中间商承担了给供应商的付款风险，就有机会在付款方式上好好谈判，为自己公司争取更小的风险。举个例子，美国Sears（美国著名零售商）直接下单给宁波的贸易公司，可能就会坚持O/A 60 days，但是同样的订单，如果Sears下给美国的进口商，付款方式不变，但是进口商再下给宁波的那家贸易公司，可能付款就变成T/T with 20% deposit, rest balanced copy of B/L（20%的订金，余款见提单复印件付清）。这里，中间商可能赚了30%的利润，但是承担了货物的品质和付款风险，因为Sears跟他们发生业务关系，不直接跟宁波的贸易公司有任何业务往来。中间商需要保证货物的品质、交期、接受60天远期的付款方式，并承担付款上的风险，甚至他们要先垫款给出口方作为订金。

国内很多出口商可能通过中间商给大买家做过几个大订单后心里就开始蠢蠢欲动，想跳过中间商直接给客户供货，缩短中间费用。但事实上，这样做有时未必能赚到更多的利润。如果你有这个想法，最好先问问自己能否接受收款的风险，能否在这个核心问题上做出让步来迁就客户？

付款方式本身就是一把双刃剑，用好了保护自己，用坏了砍伤自己，这都是有可能的。很多时候，对于新客户的开发，付款方式尤为重要，因为它决定了能否开发新客户或新市场。前期的合作不容忽视，尤其是在付款上，必须要让对方感觉到自己有足够的诚意才行。

付出是相互的，谈判的核心就是共赢。双方共同赚钱，双方各取所需，双方共担风险，这样才能让彼此都接受。

可以坚持，但不能固执；可以让步，但不能退步；可以低头，但不能输阵。这些是付款谈判的不二法则，要灵活运用，懂得变通。在为自己争取利益时能照顾到对方的感受，在给对方建议时能合理规避公司的潜在风险，这才是一个有素养的专业外贸人员应该做的。

做生意，谁都怕受骗上当，出口商会担心，进口商同样会有顾虑。所以，付款方式的选择和谈判，往往会影响业务的开展和谈判的进展。但是在谈判之前，业务人员必须了解并精通各种外贸付款方式，清楚优缺点和风险所在。这样才能心里有底，才能有针对性地和客户谈判，寻找双方能够接受的共同点。

Orders & Contracts

订单与合同专题
——注重时效，合理回复

学习目标

☆知识目标

✓了解订单和销售合同的主要内容和相关知识；
✓掌握订单和合同环节往来函电的常用表达、写作要点和基本结构。

☆能力目标

✓能够运用所学知识并结合不同场景撰写订购函和订单确认、回绝订单等环节的各类信函；
✓能够与客户就订单内容商定，并进行相应的函电沟通。

6.1 Introduction 知识介绍

6.1.1 商务知识

视频6.1

订单和合同专题学习内容包括订购函、确认函、拒绝函、订单与合同文本等内容。

订单（order）是发送给卖方，要其按协定的条件提供一定数量的商品的请求，也被称为采购单（PO）。订单既可能是买方对报盘的接受，也可能是买方主动寄发的购货单。通常是买卖双方经过发盘、还盘等一系列协商，完全同意对方的交易条件之后，由买方发送给卖方正式订单。现在许多贸易公司都使用印制好的订单文本，以确保不会疏漏任何重要的条件。

发送订单的函电为订购函。买方撰写订购函可以使用表格形式将订单内容列明在信函中，也可以附件形式发送订单的同时在信函中做简单说明。订单和订购函应注意书写清晰，语言准确，对于重要的交易条款必须做出明确规定。

卖方收到订单后通常会确认收悉。卖方可明确表示接受订单，并按照订单内容缮制合同文本且发送对方，然后双方签署，则双方订立合同并按照合同执行。或者双方直接按照订单的规定继续开展下一步行动，如按规定出货、付款等，这个环节就是订单确认与执行。

由于种种原因，如存货有限、原材料短缺、价格变动、生产能力不足、买方要求的货期太紧等，卖方有时可能会拒绝订单。此时，卖方撰写回复函时，应给出充分合理的拒绝理由，并要注意措辞和对该订单的处理方式，以免影响将来的业务关系。

国际贸易中，在订单确认环节常用的书面合同形式有合同（contract）和销售确认书（sales confirmation）。这两种文本一般由卖方拟订，经双方签字后生效，二者具有同样的法律效力。

合同是条款较完备、内容较全面的正式合同，多适用于大宗商品或成交金额较大的交易。其内容比较全面、完整，除商品的名称、规格、数量、价格、付款方式、交货期、包装、装运港、目的港、运输标识、商品检验等条件，还有异议索赔、仲裁、不可抗力等条件。

销售确认书是一种较为简单的简式合同。因其包括的条款较合同简单，所以是一种简式合同。销售确认书适用于金额不大、批数较多的交易。

6.1.2 信函结构

订购函的常用结构如下。

（1）明确主题：表达下单的意愿或说明随函附上订单。

（2）确认主要交易条件：以表格、文字或附件形式明确相关条款。

（3）结尾段：可重申重点关注的条款，如交货期、质量等。

确认/接受订购函的基本结构如下。

（1）对所收到的订单表示感谢。

（2）重申交易条件或附上销售确认书提请会签。

（3）向对方承诺照单发货或期盼继续合作。

拒绝订购函的基本结构如下。

（1）对所收到的订单表示感谢。

（2）解释原因：对不能接受订单表示遗憾并解释原因。

（3）相关建议（或有）：提供其他选择或给出建议。

（4）表达对未来业务合作的愿望。

订单和合同环节其他信函，可参考以上相应内容结构。

6.2 Task and Project 任务和项目

Task 1：撰写订单确认函

☞ 业务背景和任务

经过几次沟通并寄送样品后，浙江宁波水木毛绒玩具有限公司业务员Monica收到J. Simpson & Co., Ltd. 的Mike发来的邮件。内容如下。

例6-1：买方的订购函

Subject：Order for RX Plush Teddy Bears

Dear Monica,

Your samples of the subject goods received favorable reaction from our customers and we are pleased to enclose our Order No. JY076.

The goods are urgently needed for the Christmas promotion, so prompt delivery will be most appreciated.

Regards,

Mike

Enc.: Order No. JY076

J. Simpson & Co., Ltd.

288 North Street， Boston， USA

Tel：86-36-12345 Fax：86-36-54321

Order Form

Date： Oct. 20, 2021

Order No. JY076

Shuimu Plush Toys Co., Ltd.

Jiangbei Industrial Zone,

Ningbo, Zhejiang, 315000, China

Please supply:

Qty	Commodity	Item No.	Size	Color	Unit Price (FOB Ningbo)
500 pcs	RX Plush Teddy Bears	LH009	15 cm	pink, apple green, yellow, brown assortment	USD 1.00 per piece
1,500 pcs			25 cm	pink, apple green, yellow, brown assortment	USD 2.58 per piece
1,000 pcs			38 cm	pink, yellow, brown assortment	USD 3.06 per piece

Total: USD7,430.00

Packing: 1 pcs in a poly bag, 36 pcs. to a carton

Shipment: From Ningbo to Boston not later than Nov. 20.2021

Payment: By irrevocable sight L/C

Authorized by: Mike Smith (Manager)

Notes

1. subject goods：标题项下的货物

2. promotion：推销，促销

3. prompt：迅速的，立刻的

4. order form：订货单

☞ 写作任务

请以Monica的身份回函，表示接受订单，并随附销售确认书S/C No.SJ223，要求对方会签并寄还一份供存档。

例6-2：卖方的确认函

Subject: Order No. JY076 Accepted

Dear Mike，

视频6.2

We are pleased to inform you that we have booked your Order No.JY076 for our Plush Teddy Bears. We enclose here with our Sales Confirmation No. SJ223 in duplicate. Please countersign and return one copy for our file.

It is understood that a sight L/C in our favor will be established immediately. Meanwhile, you may rest assured that we shall effect shipment with the least possible delay upon receipt of the credit.

We appreciate your cooperation and look forward to receiving your further orders.

Best regards,
Monica

Enc.: S/C No. SJ223

水木毛绒玩具有限公司
SHUIMU PLUSH TOYS CO., LTD.
销售确认书
SALES CONFIRMATION

正本（ORIGINAL), S/C No. SJ223

兹经买卖双方同意成交下列商品，订立条款如下：

This contract is made by and agreed between the BUYER and SELLER, in accordance with the terms and conditions stipulated below.

商品名称 Commodity	货号 Item No.	数量 Quantity	尺寸 Size	颜色 Color	单价Unit Price (FOB Ningbo)	金额（美元） Amount(USD)
RX Plush Teddy Bears	LH009	500 pcs	15 cm	pink, apple green, yellow, brown assortment	USD 1.00 per pc	500.00
		1,500 pcs	25 cm	pink, apple green, yellow, brown assortment	USD 2.58 per pc	3,870.00
		1,000 pcs	38cm	pink, yellow, brown assortment	USD 3.06 per pc	3,060.00
总值TOTAL	——	3,000 pcs	——	——	——	7,430.00

TOTAL（in words): SAY US DOLLARS SEVEN THOUSAND FOUR HUNDRED AND THIRTY ONLY

Packing(包装)：1pc in a poly bag, 36 pcs. to a carton

Shipment(运输): From Ningbo to Boston within 30 days after receipt of L/C

Shipping Mark(唛头): At the seller's option

Insurance(保险): To be covered by the BUYER

Terms of payment(付款条件): By irrevocable L/C payable by draft at sight.

This contract is in TWO copies, effective since being signed/sealed by both parties.

The Buyer　　　　　　　　　　　　　　　　　The Seller

J. Simpson & Co., Ltd.　　　　　　　　　　SHUIMU PLUSH TOYS CO., LTD.

Signature:　　　　　　　　　　　　　　　　Signature:

Notes

1. book your order：接受你方订单

2. sales confirmation：销售确认书，也可写作S/C

3. in duplicate：一式两份

4. countersign：会签，连署

5. for our file：以便我方存档

6. rest assured：放心；确信

7. effect shipment：装船

8. with the least possible delay：立即，毫不耽搁

例6-1是买方发来的订单函。买方以附件形式发送订单，因此该订单函的内容较为简洁。全文共两段，每段一句话。开篇没有过多的套话，直接告知对发来的样品很满意，同时明确表示下订单。第二段是结尾段，提出对及时交货的关注。

例6-2是卖方在收到来自买方的订单函后，对于该订单进行确认，并随附销售确认书要求会签。相对买方的订单函来说，篇幅长些。全文分三段，共六句。第一段三句话，开篇同样没有多余套话，而是直接表示接受订单，并附上销售确认书一式两份，要求对方会签并返还一份。第二段用两句话对买方在订单函中关注的装运问题进行了回复，这个回复体现了专业性。结尾段用一句话表达进一步合作的愿望。

在客户的订单函中，因为涉及圣诞促销，客户对交货时间尤为关注，并且在随附的订单中，明确要求装运期不得迟于11月20日。卖方在回复客户这一要求时，并未直接表示是否可以按照客户要求的时间安排装运，而是对于信用证问题表示关注，并且承诺一收到信用证会立即安排装运，这样就将收到信用证的时间和装运问题关联在一起。

逐一对照订单与销售合同的交易条款，可以发现：除装运和支付条款二者有不同外，销售合同中的其他交易条款都是与订单一致的。对比合同与订单对应的支付条款，虽然措辞略有不同，但意思是一样的。而在装运条款中，关于装卸港口的规定，销售合同与订单内容一致。但是对于装运期的规定，订单和合同中是不同的：订单中写明装运时间在11月20日前，而合同中表述为"收到信用证后30天之内"。

信用证是一种银行承诺付款的银行信用支付方式，对卖方有较大的保障。但在实际业务中，有时买方延迟申请开立信用证，从而导致卖方执行合同时较为被动。在例6-2这个订单确认函和随附的合同中，卖方结合买方对装运期的关注，将信用证和装运环节直接关联在一起。通过这种关联来约束买方尽早提请银行开立并寄送相关信用证，以保证装运期符合买方预期，从而有利于合同的顺利履行。

Task 2：撰写订单拒绝函

☞ 业务背景和任务

2021年10月20日，浙江宁波水木毛绒玩具有限公司业务员Monica收到J. Simpson & Co., Ltd.的Mike发来的订单函（见例6-1信函），Monica立即就客户在订单中提到的交货期

问题（11月20日前）与工厂进行了沟通。工厂回复：近期订单量大增，尽管工人加紧生产，这个货期还是无法保证的。如果现在下单，预计要到12月底才能执行。

☞ **写作任务**

请以Monica的身份回函，拒绝该订单，并根据上述业务背景向客户表示歉意并解释原因。

例6-3：卖方的拒绝函

Subject: Order No. JY076

Dear Mike,

Thank you for your Order No. JY076 for 3,000 pcs of RX Plush Teddy Bears, but since you make delivery before Christmas as a firm condition, we deeply regret that we cannot supply you at present.

The manufacturers are finding it impossible to meet current demand for their stock is exhausted but consecutive new orders are pouring in. Though the workers are speeding up the production, the buyers still have to wait. Those orders placed in October are informed that they could not be dealt with until the end of December.

We are sorry that we can't meet your requirement this time. Please let us know if you need any other help, we will do our utmost to serve you.

Best regards,

Monica

Notes

1. stock：存货
2. exhausted：用完，耗尽
3. consecutive：连续不断的
4. pouring in：涌进

在国际贸易中，因客户要求的交货期与厂家出货的时间衔接问题，从而导致卖方不能接受对方订单的情况，是较为常见的。这封订单拒绝函共三段，篇幅适中。第一段首先对客户的订单表示感谢，接着明确说明因买方要求的交货期问题目前不能供货。第二段用三个长句具体解释了原因：第一句对于厂家目前的库存告罄和订单剧增情况进行陈述，第二句对于生产情况进行说明，第三句借用其他订单的执行情况来明确目前的供货周期。结尾段是两句话，表示歉意并希望对方谅解。

收到客户的订单后，首先要对订单中的各项条款逐一落实。如果确定能够顺利执行，则应尽快回复确认。如果某项条款双方存在分歧，一般应继续沟通，直至双方达成一致。订单确认一般采用确认函和随附销售合同一式两份一并发出，待对方签字并返回其中一份后，合同正式生效。如果因某种原因不能接受订单，也应尽早回复客户，表示歉意并说明原因，以取得客户的谅解。在订单拒绝函中，有时可以根据情况，给出相关建议或替代品，以供买方有更多的选择，利于今后的长远业务合作。

6.3 Actual Case Letters 实战信函

订单和合同环节的往来函电，除订单函、订单确认或拒绝函外，还有涉及订单中个别条款二次沟通的其他各类信函。具体到不同业务背景和写作习惯，函电的内容和数量差别较大。以下多封实战案例，供学习者借鉴和参考。

📹 视频6.3

例6-4：订购函

Subject: Order No. 099 for Women's Sports Wear

Thank you very much for your offer of Feb.3 and the sample for Sports Wear. We find both quality and prices satisfactory and are pleased to place an order with you for the following:

Commodity	Quantity	Size	Color	Unit Price (FOB Shanghai)
Women's Sports Wear Item No. B0712	100 pcs	small	pink, orange, light yellow assortment	USD11.64 per piece
	200 pcs	medium	pink, orange, light yellow assortment	USD11.64 per piece
	300 pcs	large	pale green, royal blue, and black assortment	USD12.00 per piece

Packing: Each piece is to be packed in a poly bag, per dozen to a tin-lined carton, and 10 dozen to a wooden case.

Other terms as per your offer of Feb.18

We expect to find a good market for the above goods and hope to place further and large orders with you in the near future.

Best regards,

Mike

Notes
1. assortment：搭配；花色品种
2. poly bag：塑料袋
3. tin-lined carton：衬锡纸箱

　　这是关于女式运动装的订购函。在收到发盘及样品后，买方对价格和质量表示满意，在来函中告知下单意图并以表格形式详细说明拟订购产品的各项要求。

例6-5：确认函

<u>Subject: Acceptance of Order No. 099 for Women's Sports Wear</u>
Dear Mike，

We are very pleased to receive your email of Feb.5 placing an order for our Women's Sport Wear.

We accordingly accept the order and shall arrange delivery as soon as possible.

We are confident that you will be completely satisfied with our goods when you received them and hope the order will lead to further business between us.

Best regards,

Monica

　　这是一封对例6-4的订购函的确认回复函，明确表示接受买方订单并将尽快安排发货。
　　在国际贸易中，如果买卖双方并非初次交易，而是之前有过合作，此时在下订单和订单确认环节时往往会简化内容和环节以提高效率。下订单时可以不随附订单附件，而是在订购函中直接列明主要条款。订单确认时也无须随附合同，只是在回函中明确表示接受订单并按相应条款执行。

例6-6：关于订单的系列函电Case 01—05

Case 01

Subject: Order No. 123 for LED Bulbs

Dear Monica,

Attached you can find the PO for 500 pcs LED bulbs.

FOB Ningbo, terms 30% deposit and balance on faxed copy of B/L.

This is a test order. Delivery required urgently.

Regards,

Mike

Notes

1. LED bulbs：LED 灯泡
2. PO：订购单
3. deposit：定金
4. balance：余款，剩余款项

Case 02

Subject: PI for Order No. 123

Dear Mike，

Thanks for the first trial order.

Regarding the payment, we need the balance before shipment for the first order.

Please find the attached PI, if you accept the payment, please send it back to me.

Regards,

Monica

Notes
PI: 形式发票

Case 03
Subject: PO for Order No. 123
Dear Monica,

50% T/T after copy of B/L is workable for us.

Attached you could find the updated PO.

Send me your PI if everything is OK.

Regards,

Mike

Notes
updated PO: 更新后的订购单

Case 04
Subject: PI for Order No. 123
Dear Mike，

My boss finally accept the payment term:
50% T/T as deposit , balance paid against the B/L faxed.

Please find the attached revised PI.

Waiting for your confirmation, thanks.

Regards,

Monica

Notes
revised PI: 修订后的形式发票

Case 05

Subject: PI confirmation for LED bulbs

Dear Monica，

Please find attached the signed PI.

The T/T for 50% will be arranged tomorrow， pls proceed ASAP.

Regards,

Mike

Notes

proceed:开始；继续进行

这是关于订单环节的一个系列案例：买卖双方就订单中的个别交易条款进行反复沟通，直至订单确认，共五封函电，文风整体较为简洁。

Case 01 是买方发出的订购函。买方对LED 灯泡下单采购，订单详情以附件形式发送，同时在信中强调了支付方式和交货期，以提请卖方重视。

Case 02 是卖方的回复函。这是卖方在收到订单函后，不同意订单中的付款条件而回复的一封还盘信。在信中，卖方提出了修改后的支付条款，并用PI（形式发票）替代S/C（销售合同）以附件发送，提请对方签字确认。

Case 03 是买方的二次订单信。买方在信中提出了一个预付50%定金的折中方案，既不是买方最先提出的30%定金，70%凭提单付款，也不是卖方要求的100%预付。

Case 04 是卖方的确认函。卖方在收到买方的二次订单信和更新后的采购单之后，表示接受的确认函，同时发送了修改后的形式发票附件提请对方确认。

Case0 5 是买方的确认函。买方在收到修改后的形式发票后，做出的确认回复。

真实环境中的贸易形势复杂多变，有时双方函电往来频繁，内容简单而直接。如果不能接受订单中的全部交易条款，也要尽快合理回复并妥善处理，积极探索可替换的折中方案，以促进交易的最终达成。

6.4 Summary 小结

在经过询盘、报价、还盘、交易细节沟通等各种往来函电之后，买卖双方进入订购和合同签约环节。本章以出口业务为主导，展示并分析了5封涉及订单和合同环节的往来函电，以及一个包含5封信函的实战系列函电，内容涵盖订购函、订单确认和拒绝订单各个环节。

订单是买方给卖方寄送的购货单，英文是order或者PO，一般是用公司的格式文本填写并以附件方式寄送，也可以用表格或文字形式列明在订购函中。卖方确认订单可以用PI或者S/C来进行回复，同时要求对方签字后返回。在当前的外贸业务中，电子合同签约，也频繁地被采用。

相关注意事项如下。

（1）订购函的内容要准确清楚。无论是随附印制订单，还是以表格或文字列明采购信息，都要注意对订购货物的描述要明确而具体，除了写明价格、数量、包装、装运、支付、保险等交易条款，还要重申己方特别关注或容易发生偏离的条款，以引起对方重视。

（2）拒绝订单要礼貌得体。如因装期问题无法接受订单，要及时回复表示歉意，并给出充分合理的理由。如因无货拒绝订单，可视情况向买方推荐合适的替代品。如因其他条款有异议而不能接受订单，可继续磋商，持续沟通或适度让步，直至达成新的订单和合同。

（3）接受订单要及时明确。接受订单函，可以用合同会签作为回复，也可仅用信函回复接受。但无论哪种方式，对于订购函表示接受的回复，都要注意表述明确且及时回复。建议采用以买方的订购函为依据，卖方拟写销售合同，然后提请双方会签来确认接受订单且合同成立。

6.5 Useful Words & Expressions 实用词汇及短语

1. order

n. & v. 订单；订货；订购

place an order with sb for sth. 向某人订购/购买某物

If you reduce your price by 5%, we will send you an order immediately. 如贵方能降价5%，我方将立即发送订单。

Please give us an idea of the quantity you wish to order. 请告知我们贵方想要订购的大致数量。

We have placed an order with you for 1,000 pcs of Men's Shirts. 我方已向你方订购1,000件男士衬衫。

trial order 试订单

accept/confirm an order 接受/确认订单

fulfill an order 执行订单

refuse an order 拒接订单

book your order = accept your order 接受订单

order form 订货单

2. sales confirmation 销售确认书（可缩写为S/C）

sales contract 销售合同；售货合同（也可缩写为S/C）

3. purchase contract 购货合同

purchase contract 可缩写为P/C。

purchase order 采购单；订购单；订单（可缩写为PO）

updated PO 更新后的订购单

4. in duplicate 一式两份

相关表述还有：

in triplicate 一式三份

in quadruplicate 一式四份

in five copies 一式五份

5. countersign

v. 会签；连署；副署

counter signature（或counter-signature，countersignature）副署签名；连署签名

When the S/C has been signed by the seller, it will be countersigned by the buyer. 销售合同经卖方签署后，须经买方会签。

Please return the duplicate completed with your counter signature. 请会签后退回一份。

6. for one's file 以便某方存档

该表述也可用 for one's records。

7. assure

v. 向……保证；使确定；使……确信

assure sb. of sth. 向某人保证某事

assure sb. that 向某人保证……

be assured of sth. 请确信某事

We assure you of the best quality and moderate prices of our goods. 请放心，我方商品质量好，价格公道。

We assure you that we shall do our best to expedite shipment. 我方保证会迅速装运。

Please be assured of our continued cooperation. 请确信我方仍将继续合作。

You may be assured that we will contact you as soon as our fresh supply comes in. 请确信一有新货到来，我方定会与贵方联系。

assure... with... 给……保险

He assured his life with that company. 他向那家保险公司投保了人寿险。

assurance

n. 保证；把握

We obtained an assurance from our regular customers that they would demand a large supply of our products. 老客户向我们保证，他们会大量求购我方产品。

assured

adj. 感到放心的

8. with the least possible delay 立即，毫不耽搁

9. assortment

n. 搭配；花色品种；分类；混合物

product assortment 产品组合

color assortment 颜色搭配

10. deposit

n. 定金

11. balance

n. 余款，剩余款项

12. PI: proforma invoice 形式发票（预开发票）

相关的短语有：

commercial invoice 商业发票

customs invoice 海关发票

consular invoice 领事发票

commercial invoice revised 修订后的形式发票

Please send us four additional copies of invoice. 请多寄送发票副本四份给我们。

13. proceed

v. 开始，继续进行

6.6 Useful Sentences 实用语句

1. Attached you can find the PO for 500 pcs LED bulbs.

附件是500只LED灯泡的订单。

2. We are glad to inform you that your samples are satisfactory, we'd like to order 4 of the items.

很高兴通知你我们对贵公司的样品感到满意，我们向你方下这类中四款的订单。

3. This is a trial order. Please send 50 sets only so that we may tap the market. If successful, we will give you large orders in the future.

试订50台，以开发市场。如果成功，随后必将大量订购。

4. We shall gladly join with you in the purchase of 100 bales of wool, to be shipped in moieties by two different vessels, to sail about a month apart.

我们很乐意协同贵公司采购100包羊毛，分两条船装运，中间间隔约一个月。

5. We have received your letter of May 23 along with your proforma invoice No. 215 in triplicate and take pleasure in placing an order with you for the said items.

我们已经收到贵方5月23日来函及第215号形式发票一式三份，现欣然向你方订购所述货物。

6. On the adjoining page we hand you an indent for various lines, which please ship at once.

我们已将委托购买的各种商品在附页列明，请立即发运。

7. Please supply the under-mentioned goods as per your quotation and samples submitted

on September 5.

请按9月5日提出的报价和样品供应下述货物。

8. 50% T/T after copy of B/L is workable for us.

我们可以接受凭提单副本支付50%货款。

9. We confirm herewith your telegraphic order of the 10th June, for 1,000 kilograms of the best sugar.

贵公司6月10日电报关于高级砂糖1,000千克订单已经收到,并予以确认。

10. We have accepted your order of March 25 for 500 typewriters.

我们已经接受3月25日500台打印机的订单。

11. We confirm supply of 1,000 pairs of shoes at the price stated in your order No.828 and will allow a 5% special discount on your order worth $5,000.

兹确认按你方第828号订单的价格供应1,000双鞋,就你方价值5,000美元或以上的订单给予5%的折扣。

12. We hereby confirm acceptance of your order and enclosing herewith our sales confirmation in two originals one of which please sign and return to us for our file.

我们特此确认接受贵方订单,并附上销售确认书正本两份,请签署其中一份并寄回我方存档。

13. We are enclosing our Sales Contract No. 55 in two originals, of which please countersign and return one copy to us for our records.

随函寄送我方55号销售合同两份正本,请会签并寄回一份供我方存档。

14. This is to confirm my telephone order of yesterday for the following items.

对我昨天电话中所联系的下列各项订货现做进一步确认。

15. In view of our heavy bookings, we are not in a position to commit ourselves to new orders.

鉴于已经收到大量预订单,我方无法承接新订单。

16. At present, we can not undertake to entertain your order owing to the uncertain availability of raw materials.

目前由于原材料的不确定性,我们不能承诺保证你方的订单。

17. We should simultaneously sign two contracts, one sales contract for soybeans, and the other contract of equal value for the purchase of cotton.

我们应同时签两份合同,一份是大豆的销售合同,另一份是等额的棉花购买合同。

18. The buyer should open an irrevocable, sight L/C in favor of the seller 30 days before the month of shipment, valid for negotiation in China until 15th days after the month of the shipment.

买方应于装运月份前30天以卖方为受益人开立不可撤销的即期信用证,到期地点在中国且在装运月后15天。

19. We could deliver the goods around 2 weeks later.

两周后我们就可以安排装运了。

20. We are working on your order and will keep you informed in course of the progress.

我们正在按照贵方订单进行运作，并将进展过程随时通知贵方。

6.7 Exercises 练习

Key 6.1

I Translate the following words and expressions into English or Chinese.

1. 会签
2. 商业发票
3. 定金
4. 销售确认书
5. 以便某方存档
6. PO
7. balance
8. PI
9. in duplicate
10. book your order

II Choose the best answer.

1. We are enclose our S/C No.200 _____ for your signature.

A. on duplicate   B. in duplicate   C. duplicate   D. to duplicate

2. We are pleased that we have booked _____ 2,000 pieces of bicycles.

A. your order   B. with you

C. an order with you   D. an order with you for

3. We assure you that any further orders you may _____ will always be carefully attended to.

A. place us   B. place with us   C. make us   D. make with us

4. We find your terms _____ and now send you our order for the following items.

A. satisfied   B. satisfaction   C. satisfactory   D. satisfy

5. The buyer suggested that many important orders _____ follow.

A. may   B. will   C. would   D. should

6. We look forward _____ your orders.

A. on   B. in   C. to   D. at

7. Attached you can find the PO _____ 500 pcs LED bulbs.

A. on   B. for   C. in   D. about

8. The ship date was 12/27 and _____ would be 1/13.

A. ETA   B. ETB   C. ETC   D. ETD

9. Please confirm the final sample, so that we can arrange _____ production ASAP.

A. large   B. all   C. other   D. mass

10. Regarding the payment, we need the _____ before shipment for the first order.

A. payment   B. cash   C. balance   D. deposit

III Translate the following sentences into English or Chinese.

1. 我方对贵方产品的质量和价格均感满意，现寄去试订单，请供应现货。

2. 随函附上我方所订 300 台 T42 型打印机的订单

3. 关于付款方式，我们对第一次订单的要求是发货前结清余款。

4. 我方很高兴发现贵方原料品质优良，现寄去 500 打雨伞的小额订单，作为试购。

5. 很遗憾因为库存不足我们不能完成你方订单。

6. FOB Ningbo, terms 30% deposit and balance on faxed copy of B/L .

7. We'd like to place an order with you for 1,000 pieces each of No.78 and No.89 at $5 and $6/FOB Ningbo respectively.

8. Your counter signature is not in agreement with the signature on the upper left corner.

9. Please find the attached PI, if you accept the payment, please send it back to me.

10. Please supply in assorted colors: preferably 6 dozen each of red, yellow, green, blue and brown.

IV Translate the following body of the letter into English.

我们已经收到贵公司的订单，非常感谢订购我们的茶叶，我们会立即予以认真办理。

请放心，该订单项下的茶叶已经用专用的茶叶包装箱细心包装好，以防运输途中受损。我们将于 7 月份之前装船发运，届时将向你方寄送装船通知和发票。

你方所提出的付款条件可以接受，你们可以完全放心，我们会迅速执行贵公司所有的订单。

现在正是茶叶的旺销季节，因而希望你们能充分利用这个良机。我们相信，你们会欣喜地从你们的客户那里听到许多对我们茶叶的赞誉，并会在你方国内为此产品打开市场。

希望以后接到贵公司更多的订单。

V Writing task.

Write a letter as per the following background and information.

经过几轮沟通，终于收到客户关于 500 件女士衬衫的订单，订单号 S123，根据订单，我们缮制了合同：S/C No.W223。

主管让你给客户 David 发一封签约函，让他们公司会签合同后尽快返回一份给我们。我方已经签好的合同一式两份，随函寄送。

6.8 Supplement & Extension 补充与拓展

大订单与小订单

外贸行业中,订单有大有小,有稳定的,有短期的,还有很多零碎的散单。客户也是一样,有长期合作的大客户,有订单一般的中小客户,也有那种有一单没一单的"游击队"客户。

作为出口行业,首先应该坚持一点,就是要一视同仁。不歧视任何客户,也不歧视任何订单。把小单做好,抓住细节,控制好品质和交期,服务到位,在订单操作过程中跟客户不断磨合,对方才会对你们公司增强信心。久而久之,供应商自身的能力和业务水平也能得到长足的提高,这个时候客户如果有大单,才能放心地交给你们。通过小订单来增强彼此的互信和配合度,将来做大单也就顺理成章了。

从个人和企业发展来看,一个成功的外贸业务员,终究是需要跟大买家打交道的,不可能仅仅依靠小订单过日子,即使利润再高,对于自身的能力和专业性来说也不会有全方位的提高,同时企业的长远发展也难以持续。

那么,如何开发大买家?如何去争取大订单呢?以下关于争取大订单的一些基本要素可供参考。

一、渠道与人脉

大买家通常都是一些大公司,且一般都有自己的采购渠道,很多不为人所知,且难以切入。而这些大买家的现有供应商,也都是从小单逐步积累起来的。

出口企业首先要做的就是尽可能多地接触不同的客户,任何机会都要把握,不要轻易错过。不仅要通过网络接触更多的潜在客户,还要多参加国内外展会,直面更多买家和渠道中间商,通过多种渠道和路径来接触到最终买家。

其次,要注重人脉建立。想要开发大买家,在一开始就要慢慢培养和建立自己的人脉。要接触尽可能多的客户、工厂、国内的同行、测试机构、外商国内采购办的员工等。只要人脉广泛,朋友介绍朋友,接触各种大买家和中间商的概率就会大大增加。人脉对于生意非常重要,而人脉的建立需要长期的积累。

二、谈判与研究

开发大买家,前期的谈判很艰难,需要相互之间的沟通和磨合,这个过程可能很长,要做好持久战的准备。同时,还可能会有无数的问题和细节要逐一地解决和确认,如大量的文书工作 (paperwork)、各种表格、每个交易环节等,这些都需要在谈判过程中顺利进行下去。任何一个细节没有把握好,都有可能使得谈判就此终结。在谈判前尽可能搜集和掌握更多的信息,才能在谈判中更加自如。

很少有客户会主动透露各种各样的信息,只能靠自己去摸索,去了解。要主动做行业和销售研究,了解对方经营的区域市场,调查渠道、零售价和竞争情况,以便能够在交易谈判中主动提出更佳的建议和方案，从而增强对潜在订单的掌控能力。

三、样品与投入

前期的投入，对于开发大买家是非常必要的，这牵涉到很多细节问题，包括打样和业务招待费等。

大买家和普通客户不同，前期可能会需要很多样品。因为大公司本身就有很多部门，有时还要拿几个给终端客户，或者拿一部分去展会看看反应。甚至有一些大买家在一开始确认样品的时候，还需要送样去第三方机构做测试，以确认品质和功能是否合乎要求等，然后再决定是否要把这个项目进展下去。

一般而言，大买家基本上不会承担样品费和寄样运费，对于一些大件产品，这些前期投入的费用可能会很惊人。此外，还有买手的实地拜访和考察等产生的接待费用。如果谈判旷日持久，这些前期费用累积起来绝对不会少。

四、验厂

大部分客户在下大订单之前，都要做一个很重要的工作，就是factory audit，也就是我们常说的验厂。

验厂非常复杂，除了人权、环评、消防、禁止雇用童工这些基本的要素外，近年又添加了诸如反恐、出入控制、商业伙伴等内容，牵涉到工厂的备料、生产、运输环节，员工的薪资、福利、培训，工厂的安全、消防、环境保护等诸多环节。这些要素都是不可忽视的。

对于第三方机构来说，一次验厂通常需要2~3天才能完成这个流程，这样才能对工厂有一个全方位的了解。

大多数的工厂都很难在第一次验厂中顺利通过，一般都会发现这样或那样的问题，需要不断地整改。而大客户也是在这个过程中了解工厂的配合程度及各方面的能力，以满足他们的要求。

五、验货

大买家的验货非常仔细，也许会派自己公司的QC（质检员），或者把这一块外包给第三方机构。

因为订单大，所以客户一般会比较仔细，一旦发现任何问题都有可能造成严重后果。特别在美国和西欧、北欧地区的发达国家，一个问题可能就会引起产品的全面recall（召回），会影响客户的公司声誉。对于一些大品牌，这会是致命的打击。

所以客户下了大单以后，对于产品各个环节的inspection（检验）会非常严格，会根据AQL（接受的质量上限）标准控制每一批货物的品质。比如pre-production inspection（产前验货），in-line inspection/DUPRO inspection（中期验货，DUPRO是during production的简写），final inspection（最终验货），甚至还需要第三方公司控制goods loading（货物装运）以确保装柜的时候小心，不会损坏产品和外箱。

以上这些是开发大买家所要具备的一些要素。一开始接触大买家难免会进退失据，谈判会发生很多问题,或者订单进行中出现各种麻烦。但这些很考验业务员的专业能力,对于一个企业的持续性发展也是大有裨益。

Chapter 7 Contract Fulfillment

履约专题
——换位思考,妥善处理

学习目标

☆知识目标

✓了解订单执行和合同履行环节的主要内容及相关知识;
✓掌握订单和合同履行相关函电的常用表述、写作要点和基本结构。

☆能力目标

✓能够运用所学知识并结合不同场景撰写生产、装运和收款等环节的各类信函;
✓能够与客户就订单执行和合同履行等环节进行相应的函电沟通。

7.1 Introduction 知识介绍

7.1.1 商务知识

视频7.1

确认订单并签订书面合同是进出口交易磋商的最后环节,合同订立标志着买卖双方磋商交易阶段的结束,而订单执行和履约环节的函电仍在继续。在这个环节和客户保持持续性的沟通,是非常必要的。这种沟通不仅有利于及时解决问题,顺利执行合同,同时也为双方今后长期的业务往来奠定基础。

就出口贸易而言,履约的程序可以归纳为货、证、船、款四个环节。结合这些环节,订单和合同履行专题学习内容包括生产情况沟通、催改证、装运通知、催款与结汇等相关函电。

货,就是备货。出口合同的履行,备货是关键。备货环节一般会涉及产前、产中和产后三个阶段,对应的函电有确认产前样品、验厂与验货、告知生产情况等内容。

证,指的是信用证,这是国际贸易中常用的一种支付方式。在备货的同时,卖方要关注信用证的开立进度和条款的审核,以免后续被动。这个环节的信函以信用证为核心,一般有催促买方尽早向银行申请开证的催证函和提请信用证条款修改的改证函。

船,指的是装运。在货物备妥后,就是按计划集港装船了。这个阶段涉及的函电有买方发出的催装函、卖方发出的装船通知等。

款,就是收款。国际贸易中多为象征性交货,即以交单代替交货,无须保证到货。在货物装运离港后,卖方拿到提单即可办理收款和结汇业务。这个阶段结合具体业务,一般有交单催款函、银行水单查询、收款通知等函电。

合同履约环节的相关函电,因内容多且杂,难以归纳统一的信函结构。这类信函因发生在履约期间,双方之前在交易磋商阶段已经有过不少沟通,彼此较为熟悉。因此,履约环节的函电,总体较为简洁,内容多为条目式排列,表意明确且具体化。

Task 1:撰写信用证改证函

☞ 业务背景和任务

宁波CJ公司收到客户8月8日开来的第LJ123号信用证,经过仔细地审核,并与合同CJ0928对照后发现三处错误:一是信用证金额有误,应为USD59,175,而不是USD59,157;二是合同允许分批装运和转船,信用证却标明不允许;三是在信用证中合同号被错写成CJ0828。

☞ 写作任务

请以宁波CJ公司业务员的身份,给客户Mike去函,要求对方立即修改信用证。

例7-1：卖方的改证函

Subject: L/C No.LJ123

Dear Mike,

Thank you for your L/C No. LJ123. On examination, we find that the following three points do not conform to the relative contract No. CJ0928:

1. The total amount of L/C should be USD 59,175 instead of USD 59,157.
2. Please amend the L/C to read: "transshipment and partial shipment allowed".
3. The contract No. is CJ0928 instead of CJ0828.

As the goods are now ready for shipment, you are requested to amend your credit ASAP. Thank you for your kind cooperation.

Best regards,

Monica

Notes

1. conform：符合，相一致
2. amend：修改
3. ASAP = as soon as possible：尽快，尽早

　　这封改证函是卖方收到信用证后，撰写的提请买方修改信用证个别条款的信函。

　　双方签约后，买方按照合同中的支付条款如期开立信用证。卖方收证后，应对照原合同认真阅读和审核信用证条款。如果在审证时发现信用证条款存在与合同内容不相符的地方，或者有一些单据要求不能满足，这时就需要修改信用证。

　　改证的程序一般是由出口商撰写改证函发给进口方，再由进口方向开证行申请修改信用证。在业务中，出口方有时会由于某些原因，不能在信用证规定的装运期内装运，这时出口方也可以撰写改证函来要求延长信用证的装运期和有效期。

　　撰写信用证改证函要注意时效性、明确性和具体化。首先，信函中应提到相关的信用证号和合同号。其次，应分条罗列出需修改的内容，并直接给出明确和具体化的修改意见，这部分要避免表意模糊和不确定。在结尾部分，应对修改的时效性加以强调，以督促进口方尽快办理相关修改业务。

Task 2：撰写装船通知

☞ **业务背景和任务**

    宁波CJ公司于9月8日在宁波港完成了合同号CJ0928项下20捆白色棉布的装船。主管让你写一封装船通知给客户Mike，告知其船名（Peace）和预计开航日期（9月10日），并随函附上一套装运单据。

☞ **写作任务**

    请以宁波CJ公司业务员的身份，结合上述信息和要求撰写装船通知。

例7-2：卖方发出的装船通知

Subject: Shipping Advice

Dear Mike,

We are pleased to inform you that 20 bales of White Cotton Cloth under S/C No. CJ0928 have now been shipped by S.S. "Peace", which will sail from Ningbo to your port on or about Sept. 10.

Enclosed is a set of shipping documents consisting of:

1. A copy of non-negotiable copy of B/L
2. A copy of signed commercial invoice
3. A copy of packing list
4. A copy of C/O
5. A copy of Insurance Policy

We hope this shipment will reach you in time and turn out to your entire satisfaction.

Best regards,

Monica

Notes

1. bale：捆
2. S/C = sales confirmation：销售确认书
3. S. S.：steamship 的缩写，也可写为S/S，后加船名，译为……号轮船
4. on or about：在某日或左右
5. shipping documents：装运单据，运输单据
 6. a copy of：一份

7. non-negotiable：不可议付的；不可流通的；不可转让的

8. B/L = bill of lading：海运提单

9. commercial invoice：商业发票

10. packing list：装箱单

11. C/O = certificate of origin：产地证

12. insurance policy：保险单

13. turn out to one's satisfaction：令人满意

　　卖方按照合同规定的装运期完成货物装运后，应及时寄送装船通知给买方。装船通知一般包括合同或订单号、商品名称、数量、金额、船名及启航日期等，以便对方及时办理或关注保险，同时做好付款和接货准备。装船通知有时也可随附或列明货物相关的装运单据。

7.3 Actual Case Letters 实战信函

　　履约阶段的往来函电，具体到不同业务情景，函电的内容各有不同。以下多封实战案例，供借鉴和参考。

例7-3：关于产前样的最后确认

Subject：Final Sample for Order No.123

Dear Mike,

The final sample has been sent to you for quality approval by UPS. The tracking number is ×××××××××.

Please confirm, so that we can arrange mass production ASAP.

Regards,

Monica

Notes

1. final sample：产前样；大货样

2. UPS：联合包裹速递服务公司，United Parcel Service Inc.

3. tracking number：快递单号

4. mass production：大货生产

例7-3的信函内容是准备产前样。

尽管在交易磋商阶段双方也是有过关于样品的寄送和确认的,但在正式生产前还是需要跟客户再次确认产前样。确认最终样品后再大批量生产,这样可以最大程度地避免彼此间的误解和麻烦。

例7-4:告知客户生产情况

Subject：Production Status for Order No.123

Dear Mike，

How are you doing?

Regarding your order No.123, we're now doing the mass production. Roughly 45% were already finished.

We could deliver the goods around 2 weeks later.

Regards,

Monica

Notes

1. production status：生产情况
2. roughly：大约,差不多

例7-4的信函是告知客户生产情况。

在收到客户的样品确认后,就要尽快安排生产了,如果是贸易商,就要马上下单给自己的供货工厂。整个生产周期因产品和数量的不同,会有极大的差异。在生产过程中,供应商要主动与客户保持沟通,适度地告知客户相关的生产情况和完成进度,尤其是生产加工时间较长的订单更要注意这个细节。

例7-5:告知客户装运情况

Subject：ETD & ETA for Order No. 123

Dear Mike，

The goods were shipped by "Hero" Vessel 1108. Please find the loading supervision photos in attachment, with container No. for your reference.

The ship date was 12/27 and ETA would be 1/13.

Regards,

Monica

Notes

1. ETD：预计离港时间
2. ETA：预计到港时间
3. loading supervision photos：港口监装照片
4. ship date：开船日

例7-5的信函是告知客户装运情况。

在货物备妥后，就是按计划集港装船了。这时候，要告知客户具体的航次和预计的到港时间，以便让客户掌握具体情况，及时联系目的港的货代，安排货物在当地的清关、运输及其他进口手续。这类信函，也是业务中经常提到的装船通知。

例7-6 申请验厂

Subject：Application for Factory Audit

Dear Jack，

Glad to write to you.

Our customer Mike in USA gave me your contact information.

We got their order for sports wear and will deliver the goods roughly 2 weeks later.
My client asked me to apply the factory evaluation. Please help to arrange it.
Next Monday to Wednesday is OK for us. Please advise if acceptable.

Best regards,

Monica

Notes

1. factory audit：验厂
2. evaluation：评价，评估

例7-6的信函是卖方申请第三方验厂的邮件。

很多大客户和专业客户,在下了订单之后,一般都是要进行验厂的,目的是了解供应商的真实情况,以便对未来的订单做出选择。尤其是大订单,对于供应商自己的工厂或者上游工厂的要求是非常高的。只有第三方出具的专业报告,才能让他们对供应商有一个大致的了解。

验厂又叫工厂审核,俗称查厂,简单地理解就是检查工厂。验厂主要是考察工厂的生产实力、安全生产、操作规范等。验厂的内容一般分为人权验厂、品质验厂和反恐验厂。具体就是从社会责任、质量技术和供应链安全等方面,依据一定的标准对工厂进行审核或者评估。企业"验厂"活动已经在中国的出口企业中普及,接受跨国公司和中介机构"验厂"对我国出口生产企业,尤其是纺织和服装、玩具、日用品、电子和机械等劳动密集型企业几乎成为必须满足的条件。

关于申请验厂的邮件,有一个要点要特别注意:这种邮件在发送给查验方提出验厂或验货申请的时候,一定不要忘记抄送环节。比如,例7-6这封信,就要同时抄送给客户Mike,也就是这笔订单的采购方。

例7-7:交单并催款

Subject：Shipping Documents and Copy of B/L

Dear Mike,

All the bearings you ordered were shipped last Thursday. Attached you can find the invoice, packing list and copy of B/L.

The ETA is September 28, to Auckland.

Please help to settle the rest payment USD 70,000 to our bank account soon.

Thanks & best regards,

Monica

例7-8:装运及催款函

Subject: Asking for Payment

Dear Mike,

We wish to inform you that the consignment under S/C No. JR108 has been shipped yesterday via S.S. "Hero". We wish the goods would reach you in good condition.

Now we fax the copy of B/L to you, and remind you to make the balance of payment within one week. Once we receive your payment, the B/L and other documents will be sent by Express.

Please let us know when you have settled the payment.

Regards,

Monica

    例7-7和例7-8的信函都是卖方在完成装运后，向买方发出的催款函。

    在国际贸易中，不同的收汇方式，装运后单据处理的方式也不同。以托收和信用证方式结汇，单据需要提交银行。以汇付方式收款，由出口方自行寄送单据给进口方。出货后，卖方应及时提交相关单据给客户并催款。单据包中的提单是物权凭证，在寄送和处理时要慎重对待。一般是凭提单副本向买方证明已交货并催款，然后等顺利收款后，再寄送提单正本以便买方提货。即使是信用证或托收之类的付款方式，在单据提交银行后，也应另行寄送或随附一套副本单据给客户参考，并告知货已装运发出。

例7-9：请客户查询并提供银行水单

Subject：Payment Problems

Dear Mike,

I'm sorry to inform you that we haven't received your payment.

Could you kindly re-check it? Please also send us the bank receipt for record.

Best regards,

Monica

    例7-9的信函是卖方就收款问题发出的询问函。

    有些时候，卖方已经通知客户付款，但是一直没见到款项到位。这个时候，应主动询问客户，让对方帮忙查询，或者提供银行水单。

例7-10：收款通知

Subject: Payment Received with Thanks

Dear Mike,

We have received the payment for the shipped 3 orders.

Thank you very much for your support and trust. We're immensely delighted to get these projects.

Hope we could expand our current business in the near future.

Best regards,

Monica

例7-10的信函是卖方在收到款项后向买方发出的通知函。

在国际贸易中，卖方收到货款后，需要在第一时间通知客户，并表示感谢。这不仅是基本的礼貌，也是为了节约客户的时间，避免客户把精力花在跟财务或银行确认是否电汇成功上。在平时工作中，一旦客户告知货款已经安排，就应及时查询己方的银行账户，看是否有款项入账。

7.4 Summary 小结

本章以出口业务为引导，突出实用性特色，展示并分析了涵盖订单执行和合同履行相关环节的10封信函。按照执行订单的一般业务程序，具体内容包括改证函、产前样品确认函、告知生产情况、装船通知、申请验厂函、催款与收汇函等。

这类函电在撰写时要注意用词的专业性和准确性，要明确地表达主题和清晰地陈述事实，是关于催证、改证，还是告知装运情况或催款等。

合同履约环节要注意换位思考和妥善处理，体现业务素质和专业性。要能够学会用客户的眼睛来关注订单的执行，及时告知客户订单完成的进度和最新的消息。在合同履行中的细致、周到和换位思考，会对以后双方之间的长远业务发展奠定一个良好的基础。

7.5 Useful Words & Expressions 实用词汇及短语

1. on examine 经检验
类似的表述：on perusal, after checking

2. amend

v. 修改

修改信用证可以说 amend/modify/adjust the L/C

amend sth. to read… 将……修改为……

Please amend the amount of the L/C to read "5% more or less allowed". 请将信用证金额修改为：允许5%的上下浮动。

amendment

n. 修改；修改书

make amendment to sth.

You are requested to make amendment to L/C No.89 without delay. 要求你方立即修改第89号信用证。

3. discrepancy

n. 差错；差异；不符点

After checking, we found there are some discrepancies in the L/C. 经审核，我方发现信用证中存在不符点。

4. insert

v. 插入

Please insert the clause "Transshipment at Hong Kong". 请增加"在香港转船"的条款。

如需要删除某条款，可用"delete"。

Please delete the clause "by direct steamer". 请删除"直达船"的条款。

5. extend

v. 延伸；延展

extend…to… 将……延长至……

Please extend the validity of L/C to August 10. 请将信用证的有效期延展至8月10日。

extension

n. 延期

make extension of the L/C 延展信用证

6. express regret to sb. for/about/over/at sth. 因某事向某人致歉

We express our regret to you for delay in shipment. 我方因延迟装运向你方深表歉意。

7. DUPRO inspection

DUPRO inspection是during production inspection的简写，意思是在生产过程中的检验和查验，即产中验货。

final inspection 完货后检验

其他相关表述：

FE = factory evaluation 验厂

factory audit 验厂

The factory audit is must. 验厂是强制的。

I don't think re-inspection is needed. 我认为重验没有必要

8. production status 生产情况

expedite the production 加快生产进度

9. ETD

ETD = estimated time of departure 预计离港时间

cargo cut-off date 截关日

ship date 开船日

ETA = estimated time of arrival 预计到港时间

10. loading supervision photos 港口监装照片

11. non-negotiable 不可议付的；不可流通的；不可转让的

12. ASAP = as soon as possible 尽快；尽早

ASAP也可写作asap。

13. S. S.

S. S. 是steamship 的缩写，也可写为S/S，后加船名，译为……号轮船。

via S.S. "Peace" 经由"和平号"货轮运输

14. pay in advance 预付

pay by installment 分期付款

full payment 全额付款

15. bank receipt 银行款流水单；银行水单

16. conclude the business 成交，完成交易

17. turn out to one's satisfaction 令人满意

18. final sample 产前样；大货样

19. UPS 联合包裹速递服务公司，即United Parcel Service Inc.

20. tracking number 快递单号

7.6 Useful Sentences 实用语句

1. We regret that we could not ship the goods by a March vessel only because of the delay of your L/C. Please attend to this matter with all speed.

我方感到遗憾，由于贵方信用证延误，我方的货不能装3月份的船，请尽快解决此问题。

2. It is seasonal items, and you couldn't deliver them late, even 1 week.

这是季节性产品，无论如何您都不能延期交货，一个星期都不可以。

3. We will charge you 10% if you delay more than 2 shipments.

如果你延迟2个船期交货，我们会扣款10%。

4. The equipment will be ready for shipment by the end of this month, please notify us at an early date of the name of the chartered steamer and its date of arrival at our port.

设备到本月底将备好待运，请早日通过我方租船船名和抵达我港日期。

5. If you would like to arrange the goods by air delivery, you have to pay for the freight charge in advance.

如果你想要我们安排空运，请事先把运费支付给我们。

6. The final sample will be sent to you after quality approval.

样品经品质确认后，我们会寄给您最终的大货样。

7. Please use brown mail order box as packaging. All the cartons should be passed the drop test.

请使用棕色邮购盒包装。所有的外箱都必须经受摔箱跌落测试。

8. If you would like to delay the FE, we have to charge you the additional cost.

如果你方想延期验厂，我们不得不征收额外费用。

9. We are glad to inform you that an L/C amounting to US$20,000 has been established in your favor, valid up to May 18.

很高兴地通知贵方，本公司已经开立一份金额为2万美元的信用证，以贵方为受益人，有效期至5月18日。

10. We could book 1×40'GP, and the other goods will be shipped by LCL.

我们会订一个40尺整柜，剩下的部分就走散货。

11. You are requested to notify your client to increase the L/C amount to USD578,000.

要求你们通知贵方客户将信用证金额增加到57.8万美元。

12. I have to do the inspection after 100% completed.

我们必须等产品全部完成后才能开始验货。

13. After our re-work for packaging, I'm sure we could pass the drop test this time.

我们重新做了包装，我相信这次一定能通过摔箱测试。

14. We enclose a cheque in partial payment for the goods shipped on consignment.

随函附寄支票一张，作为所运来的寄售货物的部分款项。

15. Enclosed please find the invoice of eighty bales cotton bought by your order, and shipped to Kobe per "Peace", as per the enclosed B/L.

根据贵公司的订单，已将80包棉花装于驶往神户的和平号货轮，随函寄去发票及提单各一份，请查收。

16. We have not yet received the remainder of payment for PO J-31.

我们尚未收到贵方关于订单号J-31的余款。

17. We have surrendered to the Bank of China, Ningbo, the clean, shipped on board B/L in complete set together with other documents according to the terms of your L/C No.289.

我们已根据贵方第289号信用证条款，将全套清洁提单连同其他单据提交中国银行宁波分行。

18. The original shipping documents have been presented to the negotiating bank here for payment.

装船单据正本已提交这里的议付行以支付货款。

19. We were pleased to receive your bank check. It has been credited to your account, which in now completely clear.

很高兴收到贵方的银行汇票。我们已将此款记入贵公司账户的贷方，现已完全结清。

20. Enclosed we hand you a statement of account to date, showing a balance of USD 20,000 in our favor, which we trust will be found in order.

到目前为止，我公司应收账款尚有2万美元。兹奉上结算报告一份，敬请查收为荷。

7.7 Exercises 练习

I Translate the following words and expressions into English or Chinese.

Key 7.1

1. 预计离港时间
2. 预计到港时间
3. 港口监装照片
4. 完货后检验
5. 截关日
6. pay by installment

7. final sample

8. asap

9. conclude the business

10. Factory audit

II Choose the best answer.

1. We wish to point out that stipulations in the relative L/C must be strictly conform to the stated in our S/C so as to avoid _____ the L/C subsequently.

    A. amend   B. amendment   C. amending   D. to amend

2. It is understood that a L/C in our favor _____ the _____ shoes should be opened immediately.

    A. covering; saying   B. covered; said

    C. covered; saying   D. covering; said

3. You may rest _____ that we will effect shipment without delay on receipt of your L/C.

    A. insured   B. ensured   C. issued   D. assured

4. Your drafts must be accompanied by the following documents, _____ are to be delivered to us against our acceptance of the draft.

    A. what   B. that   C. which   D. while

5. We wish to draw your attention _____ the L/C covering your order No.158 has not reached us.

    A. to the fact that   B. to that   C. to   D. that

6. Taking into consideration our long-standing business relations with you, we accept _____ by D/P.

    A. enquiries   B. invitations   C. installment   D. payment

7. We regret that we have suffered heavy loss _____ your improper packing.

    A. resulted from   B. resulting from   C. resulted in   D. resulting in

8. The stipulations of the L/C should _____ those of the contract.

    A. agree to   B. agree in   C. agree on   D. agree with

9. We must point out that _____ your L/C reaches us before the end of this month, we shall not be able to effect shipment within the stipulated time limit.

    A. if   B. unless   C. in case   D. in case of

10. You are authorized to draw a 60 days draft _____ our bank _____ this credit _____ the amount of your invoice.

    A. on; against; for   B. against; on; for

    C. for; against; on   D. against; for; one

III Translate the following sentences into English or Chinese.

1. 随函附上有关货物的装运单据一套。

2. 贵方信用证的所有条款都必须与合同条款一致。

3. 这是根据您修改过的订单所做的形式发票。

4. 你们能提供门到门服务吗？

5. 产前样品已经通过联合包裹寄出供您方确认。

6. Please amend L/C No. 526 allowing transshipment and partial shipment, so that we may effect shipment without delay.

7. Please find the loading supervision photos in attachment, with container No. for your reference.

8. All banking charges，including discrepancy fee and any wire commission will be deducted from the proceeds.

9. Please note that your deposit is past due.

10. With regard to L/C No.705, we have already instructed the opening bank to extend the date of shipment and validity to May 15 and May 30 respectively.

IV Translate the following body of the letter into English.

两万美元已经收到，非常感谢。

随函附上我们的生产安排表，以供参考。这批货物将于10月20日前备妥。在生产期间，我会定期给您发照片。如果这期间没有收到照片，请给我发邮件。

另一方面，请马上寄送您的商标或品牌其他图片给我们，以便我们制作透明的不干胶贴纸并将贴纸粘贴在包装盒上。

有任何问题,请联系我。

V Writing task.

Write a letter as per the following background and information.

宁波某公司合同号为JR003项下的货物已于昨日装载和平号货轮装运。按照之前双方约定,货物装运后需凭提单复印件支付余款。

主管让你将提单复印件发个传真给客户Black Jones,同时写封邮件,催促其要在收到提单复印件后一周内支付余款。在收到余款后,就把提单和其他单据一并快递给客户。

这个客户的一贯作风是有点拖延,主管嘱咐你,要将延迟付款的后果讲清楚:如果没在一周内收到余款,我们就会通知货代中止装运,所有后果由客户自负。如果客户付款了,也请他通知我们一下。

7.8 Supplement & Extension 补充与拓展

各国交易习惯小知识

对于外贸从业人员来说,了解买家的习惯,在交易中对不同买家采取恰当的态度,提出不同的交易条件,非常重要。这一方面将有效提高成交量,另一方面也能够避免不必要的损失。以下是一些外贸从业人员近年摸索出来的全球部分买家的采购习惯,仅供参考。

1. 俄罗斯:交易合同大多以T/T成交,签约后一般要求必须准时出货,很少开L/C。中俄市场有一定的潜力,但客户拓展渠道效果一般,其中以展会联系或深入当地拜访较为有效。当地语言以俄语为主,英语沟通受限,一般需要专业翻译协助。

2. 美国:交易条件较为成熟和多样化,出口美国的中国产品数量多,订单大,但整体利润较低。

3. 墨西哥:一般不接受L/C即期付款条件,但接受L/C远期付款。订单量普遍较小,一般要求看样订货。

注意事项:墨西哥政府规定,所有电子产品的进口都必须事先向墨西哥工商部申请质量标准证书 (NOM),即符合美国UL标准,方允许进口。对墨西哥出口产品的交货期尽量不要太长,首先需尽量满足条件及有关规定,其次需提高产品质量和档次。

4. 东欧:该市场有其自身特点。产品要求的档次不高,但要想求得长期发展,质量不佳的大路货没有潜力。

5. 中东:习惯通过代理商间接交易,对直接交易表现冷淡。相对于日本、欧、美国等地而言对产品要求不是很高。比较重视颜色,偏好深色物品。订单固定但利润小,量不大。

注意事项:要特别小心代理商,避免被对方进行多形式的压价。更应注意遵循一诺千金的原则。合同、协议一经签字,就应履约尽责,哪怕是口头允诺的事也要尽力做。同时应重视客户的询价。保持良好态度,别太在几件样品或样本邮寄费上斤斤计较。

6. 非洲:看货买卖,一手交钱,一手交货,或赊销、代销。订单量小,品种多,要货急。

注意事项：非洲国家实行的进出口商品装船前检验，在实际操作中有时会增加我方费用或延误交货期。

7. 南非：信用卡、支票使用普遍，习惯"先消费后付款"。

注意事项：因资金有限，银行利率高，仍习惯于见货付款或分期付款，一般不开即期信用证。

8. 摩洛哥：常采取低报货值，差价现金支付的方式交易。

注意事项：摩洛哥进口关税水平普遍较高，外汇管理较严。D/P方式在对该国出口业务中存在较大的收汇风险。

9. 丹麦：丹麦进口商在与国外出口商做第一笔生意时，一般愿意接受信用证的支付方式。此后，通常使用凭单付现和30~90天远期付款交单或承兑交单。一开始多为小金额订单，如样品寄售或试销性订单。

注意事项：要求货样一样，很注重交货期。在履行一个新合同时，出口商应明确具体的交货期，并及时完成交货义务。任何违背交货期，导致延期交货的，都有可能被丹麦进口商取消合同。

10. 西班牙：接受远期信用证交付货款，但赊账期一般为90天，一些大型连锁店的采购账期长达150天。

注意事项：该国对其输入产品不收关税。供应商应缩短生产时间，注重品质及商誉。

索赔与售后专题
——保持沟通，着眼未来

学习目标

☆知识目标

✓了解索赔处理与售后跟进环节的主要内容和相关知识；

✓掌握索赔处理与售后跟进相关函电的常用表述、写作要点和基本结构。

☆能力目标

✓能够运用所学知识并结合不同场景撰写处理索赔和客户维护等各类函电；

✓能够与客户就售后各环节进行相应的函电沟通。

8.1 Introduction 知识介绍

8.1.1 商务知识

经过交易磋商和合同履行环节,业务接近尾声。索赔与售后专题学习内容包括索赔函,理赔函,售后跟进、推介新品、节日问候等相关函电。

1. 索赔与理赔

在执行合同的过程中,签约双方都应该履行合同义务。如果任何一方未能全部或部分履行自己的义务,即构成"违约"。一旦发生这种情况,受损方有权根据合同要求责任方赔偿或是采取补救措施。受损方采取的这种行动称之为"索赔"(claim);责任方就受损失一方提出的要求进行处理,即是"理赔"(settlement)。

索赔时,应根据事实和有关证明分清责任,向责任方、轮船公司或保险公司提出索赔;理赔时,应根据事实和有关证明,该赔则赔,不该赔则拒绝赔偿。进出口业务中,较多的情况是买方就质量、数量、包装或交货问题向卖方索赔。但如果买方出现迟开信用证或延迟付款等问题,卖方也会提出索赔。

除此之外,有时也会有保险索赔和运输索赔。前者是当保险合同承保范围内的风险发生并造成货物损失时,向保险公司提出索赔;后者是当因运输公司的过错而引起货物受损时,向运输公司提出索赔。

2. 售后服务与推介新品

在合同顺利履约和安全收款后,建立客户档案并保持后续联系,是尤为重要的。

产品销售后需要及时跟进了解后续进展,这是维系长期贸易关系的有效手段。主动联系客户,询问产品的使用情况或在当地市场的销售情况,一方面可以让客户知晓我方对他的关注,另一方面也便于把握对方的采购频率。

当公司有促销活动、新品上市或对老产品进行更新换代时,也应在第一时间及时通知老客户。让这些老客户时刻有VIP的感觉,享受到在别的供应商那里享受不到的特殊待遇。

各种节日的问候也是必不可少的。每逢节日或者客户的生日,可以发送问候短函并寄送一些小礼品,来维系与客户的感情。

在实际业务中,要结合具体情况妥善把握这些售后联系的频率和内容,避免对客户造成困扰和不便。

8.1.2 信函结构

索赔函的正文内容结构一般包括如下几部分。

(1)概述收货情况并提出索赔。

(2)说明索赔的原因以及由此产生的问题或造成的损失。

(3)提出解决索赔的建议或要求。

(4)其他或督促。

理赔函的正文内容结构一般包括如下几部分。

（1）对该索赔事件表示遗憾或道歉。

（2）解释出现的原因并表明立场（同意或不同意索赔）。

（3）提出解决问题的建议。

（4）表达期望。

售后函措辞一般都比较随意，如同朋友间的日常联络，正文内容一般包括：问候、询问和了解产品销售情况、推介新品或告知促销活动等

8.2 Task and Project 任务和项目

Task 1：撰写理赔函—接受

☞ 业务背景和任务

浙江宁波水木纺织品有限公司9月18日收到德国JK公司发来的索赔函（见例8-1），申诉错发货物。经调查，由于数字混淆，包装中确实出现差错。公司迅速补发了正确的货物，并完成相关单据的制作。

例8-1：买方的索赔函1

Subject：Our Order No. 233

Dear Monica，

We duly received the documents and took delivery of the goods on arrival of s/s "Lucky" at Hamburg.

Thank you for your prompt execution of this order. Everything appears to be correct and in good condition except in case No.9.

Unfortunately when we opened this case, we found it contained completely different articles, and we can only presume that a mistake was made and the contents of this case were for another order.

As we need the articles we ordered to complete deliveries to our own customers, we must ask you to arrange for the dispatch of replacements at once. We attach a list of the contents of case No.9 and shall be glad if you will check this with our order and the copy of your invoice.

In the meantime, we are holding the above-mentioned case at your disposal. Please let us know what you wish us to do with it.

Best regards,

John

Notes
1. prompt execution：及时执行
2. contents of this case：箱内所装货物
3. replacement：替代物
4. at your disposal：任你处理

☞写作任务
请以Monica的身份撰写理赔函。对于己方差错表示歉意，并告知对方货物已经补发，有关单据将在两日内寄出。同时希望对方能暂时保管错发的货物，等待我方在当地的运输代理行"环球运输公司"派人前往处理。

例8-2：卖方的理赔函

Subject：Your Order No. 233 per S/S "Lucky"
Dear John,

Thank you for your email of Sept. 18th. We are glad to know that the consignment was delivered promptly, but it was with great regret that we heard case No. 9 did not contain the goods you ordered.

On going into the matter, we find that a mistake was indeed made in packing, through a confusion of number, and we have arranged for the right goods to be dispatched to you at once. Relative documents will be mailed within two days.

We will appreciate it if you will keep case No. 9 and contents until called for by the local agents of World Transport Ltd., our forwarding agents, whom we have instructed accordingly.

Please accept our many apologies for the inconvenience caused by our mistakes.

Best regards,

Monica

Notes

1. consignment：货物

2. on going into the matter：经调查此事

3. called for：拜访，请求，要求

4. forwarding agents：运输代理

5. accordingly：相应地，照着办

例8-1的信函是买方发来的索赔函。全文五段，共八句话。第一段对于到货情况进行概述；第二段和第三段对于货物被错发的问题进行具体描述；第四段提出了解决方案；结尾段体现买方的配合态度。

例8-2的信函是卖方在收到买方的索赔函后，确认接受索赔并积极处理后回复的理赔函。全文四段，共六句。第一段感谢客户来函，并对索赔事件表示遗憾；第二段解释并回复客户的索赔要求；第三段是关于相关的后续处理请求；结尾段再次表达歉意。

在国际贸易中，索赔虽然不是在每笔交易中都涉及，但还是时有发生。有时损失不大，受损方不一定会为了补偿而提出索赔。但是，可能会撰写一封申诉（投诉）信或说明函，告知对方相关情况，避免类似事情再次发生。

不管是申诉信还是索赔函，写信人都要注意措辞和表意，要清晰地陈述事实，不可咄咄逼人。在处理申诉或索赔时，应仔细调查并厘清责任，遵循有理有据的原则，及时地予以回复。

Task 2：撰写索赔回复函

☞业务背景和任务

浙江宁波水木纺织品有限公司10月18日收到德国JK公司发来的索赔函（见例8-3），就产品质量不达标提出索赔。经详细调查，宁波公司发送的货物是按照对方提供的样品生产的，并且完全符合要求，大货与样品两者的质量完全相同。因此，宁波水木纺织品公司回函拒绝客户的索赔要求。

例8-3：买方的索赔函2

Subject：Our Order No. J276

Dear Monica,

We have duly received the goods of our Order No. J276 for Cotton Jacquard Bath Towels. However, we regret to say that the goods we received are not up to our standard, and they are quite unsalable in this market.

Needless to say, we have suffered a great loss and the inferior quality of the lot put us in to great trouble, for our end users refused to accept these goods, and they are going to seek for other resources.

Under these circumstances, we have to make a claim with you as follows:

Claim Number	Claim for	Amount
CM-90123	Quality	US$ 235,300

We feel sure that you will give our claim your most favorable consideration, and let us have your settlement at an early date.

Regards,

John

Notes

1. Cotton Jacquard Bath Towels：棉质提花浴巾

2. unsalable：卖不掉的；无销路的

3. needless to say：不用说

4. inferior：（质量等）差的，次的，劣等的

☞ **写作任务**

　　请以 Monica 的身份撰写回复函拒绝客户的索赔要求。对于拒绝索赔的原因进行解释，并明确表示，因货物是按照对方提供的样品进行生产的，且符合要求，因此对于货物不宜在贵方市场销售，不予承担责任。同时希望客户能撤回索赔要求，以使双方未来的交易不受影响。

例 8-4：卖方拒绝索赔的回复函

Subject：Your Claim on Order No. J276

Dear John,

With reference to your claim on Order No. J276 for inferior quality, we have looked into this matter in details and so far as we have found that there is no ground for such a claim to be lodged against us.

If you can examine the goods with great care with the sample, you will find they are of the exactly same quality. Since the goods are manufactured according to you supplied sample and all your requirements are complied with, we assume no responsibility whatsoever if you now find them unsuitable for sale in your market.

As we are in no way liable for the quality of the goods, we regret being unable to entertain your claim.

We hope our explanation will convince you to withdraw you claim and hope this matter will have no harmful effect on the dealings between us in future.

Best regards,

Monica

Notes

1. there is no ground for…：是毫无根据的；是站不住脚的
2. assume：承担；担任
3. whatsoever：无论什么

　　例8-3的信函是买方就货物的质量问题发来的索赔函，全文共四段。第一段概述到货情况，同时明确说明产品不符合质量标准；第二段解释因产品质量问题造成的损失和问题；第三段提出了具体索赔方案；结尾段表达期望。

　　例8-4的信函是卖方在收到买方的索赔函后，经过调查后拒绝赔付买方的回函，全文也是四段。第一段针对买方的索赔告知己方调查后的结论；第二段解释说明不能负责的原因；第三段用一句话明确告知不接受索赔要求；结尾段表达期望。

　　收到客户的索赔要求后，要详细调查并妥善处理。既不能推卸责任，也不能一味让步。在遇到无理索赔时，要据理力争，陈述原因，拿出证据，不能简单地拒绝，更不能随意用赔钱来解决一切。

8.3 Actual Case Letters 实战信函

　　索赔与售后环节的往来函电，除索赔函和理赔函外，还有涉及保持联络和提供服务的售后跟进、推介新品、节日问候等其他各类信函。以下多封实战案例，供学习者借鉴和参考。

视频8.1

例8-5：卖方的理赔函—替代方案

Subject：Compensation Alternatives

Dear Mike,

We would like to express our deeply regret that the barcode for 10% goods couldn't be scanned. It is too expensive to do the re-work in UK.

We'll give you another 10% goods by air as replacement. Is it acceptable to give us 20 days? If time limited, we suggest you try our new model KJ-95. We have stock for this item, and the quality is better than your order KJ-94. These products could be delivered in 3 days after package.

Please give us your comments soon.

Best regards,

Monica

Notes
1. compensation：补偿；赔偿
2. barcode：条形码
3. re-work：二次加工；返工
4. comments：评论；意见

    例8-5的信函的业务场景：客户收到货物后，发现部分产品包装上的条形码扫不出来，从而导致货物不能够直接上货架，于是向供应商提出索赔要求。

    在接到这封索赔函后，供应商内部紧急商讨了几种解决方式。第一种是寄送一批条形码不干胶给客户，让客户安排返工重贴，但这里有个费用和人工成本问题需要跟客户二次商讨。第二种是另行空运10%的货品，但这样需要20天的生产和装运周期。第三种是用另一型号的库存产品来替代，这样3天内可发货。第四种是供应商自行联系并安排第三方公司在当地负责条码不干胶重贴的返工事宜。通过与第三方公司联系得知，当地人工成本过高且加工时效无法保证。于是，供应商就其中的第二和第三方案回复客户，撰写理赔函。

    这封理赔函是一篇三段论，第一段用两句话概述了对方的索赔诉求，同时为下面的解决方案做出引导。第二段共五句话，分述了两种解决方案，以供选择。第三段用一句话结尾，督促客户尽快作出决定。

    这封针对买方索赔的回函，行文流畅，措辞严谨。对于客户提出的索赔问题，并没有做更多地解释和说明，而是专注解决问题，并同时提供了两种不同的方案，供客户选择。

例8-6：卖方的回复函——拒绝索赔

Subject：Compensation Refusal

Dear Mike,

We won't accept your request for compensation. It is not our responsibility.
According to your PO, we should do the mass production the same as your sample. That means,

we handled the OEM order for you. You already confirmed our samples and inspected all the products.

We're so sorry to hear that all the products should be recalled due to the patent issue in Germany. However, you're our customer, and you're the German importer. You should pay attention to these problems when placing orders. It is your duty to check the issue, not us.

We really hope you could understand our position.

Best regards,

Monica

Notes
1. OEM: 代工生产
2. recalled: 召回
3. patent issue: 专利问题

　　例8-6的信函的业务场景：货物在当地因为专利问题被下架（召回），买方据此提出索赔。收到客户的索赔信后，卖方经过认真地分析，决定对这个索赔要求拒绝赔付。
　　处理索赔的信函，因为要陈述事实，提出解决方案，同时还要注意措辞和细节表意，一般来说，篇幅不会特别短。这封函电全文四段，共十句话。第一段，没有任何客套和迂回，直接陈述了主题：我们拒绝赔付。第二段和第三段是解释和说明，明确责任归属。结尾段表达期望。这封拒绝索赔的信函，结构完整，理由充分。
　　在有些情况下，客户只是以为责任是供货商的，就开始索赔。在处理这类索赔要求的时候，一定要注意充分沟通，摆事实讲道理，让客户明白原因和真相，以协商和沟通来解决问题。

例8-7：询问采购计划

Subject: New Purchase Plan
Dear Mike,

Long time no see!

It has been 3 months since we concluded our last transaction. I would like to check with you about the distribution and retail status of our plush toys in your market so as to perfect the patterns and the quality of them.

Do you have other suggestions for our products? I would like to know if you have some new purchasing plans or programs?

Best regards,

Monica

Notes
1. conclude: 完成
2. transaction: 交易; 买卖
3. distribution: 分销; 批发
4. retail status: 零售情况
5. purchasing plan: 采购计划

例8-7的信函是一封发给老客户的售后函, 想要了解对方是否有新的采购意向。

产品销售以后, 是需要跟进了解销售进展的。比如产品在当地市场的销售情况如何? 有哪些需要改进的地方? 跟市场上同类产品相比有什么优缺点? 等等。这些沟通对于未来的订单会很有帮助。

这种与老客户之间的售后函, 一般措辞都比较随意自然, 如同朋友间的日常联络。生意其实就是一种沟通, 保持联系是沟通的前提。

例8-8: 推介新品

Subject: CRV Screwdriver Bits Kit
Dear Mike,

Sorry to trouble you at the moment. I would like to check with you about your last order for 56 pcs CRV screwdriver bits kit. Have you sold them out?

Now we developed a similar set, and used carbon steel, instead. The pricing could be roughly 30% lower. We plan to do a promotion in Holland this June. Do you have interest in this set?

Best regards,
Monica

Notes
1. screwdriver bits kit: 螺丝刀工具套装
2. carbon steel: 碳钢

例8-8的信函的业务场景：客户之前采购了一批螺丝刀工具套装，公司目前推出了一款新的螺丝刀套装，材质不同，价格便宜。于是，卖方给客户发函告知此事并推介新品。

当产品更新换代或者有新产品推出时，供货商应该第一时间通知老客户。一方面，可借此保持持续沟通的频率，增加客户黏性。另一方面，也是提请客户注意，及时调整在当地市场的营销策略，以免受到同类新品的冲击影响现存货品的销售。

例8-9：告知促销活动

Subject：Details about the Latest Catalog

Dear Mike ,

Nice to contact you.

In order to celebrate the 10-year-anniversary of our company, we currently are offering 20% discount of all-line products for returning customers like you.

Please call me before 20th this month to take advantage of the limited time offer. Attached is our latest catalogs for your reference.

Looking forward to doing business with you again soon and good time for you.

Best regards,

Monica

Notes
1. 10-year-anniversary：十周年纪念
2. all-line products：全线产品

如果公司有节日或庆典等促销活动，需要及时联络老客户，告知相关的活动时间和折扣情况，以便于客户优先选购。

周到适当的售后函对未来的订单，对买卖双方长期的业务发展是非常重要的。

8-10：节日问候

Subject：New Year Greetings

Dear Mike,

Holiday greetings and best wishes for the New Year! May you and your family members have a joyous holiday season.

Thank you for your great supports for our company's products over the past few years and I hope we will enjoy a better cooperative relation in the coming year.

Please note that I will not be in office during Jan. 1st–3rd, due to the New Year holiday. For any questions, please call my mobile or send me message online.

Best regards,

Monica

Notes

1. joyous：欢乐的，令人愉快的
2. message online：在线消息

　　跟老客户保持持续性联络，做好客户维护，是外贸业务中非常重要的环节。

　　售后函中除了关于产品和促销活动的商务沟通，各种节日的问候也是必不可少的。每逢节日，可以发送问候信函或寄送一些小礼品，维系与客户的感情。

　　在拓展新客户的同时，维系好老客户，建立稳定的客户群，一方面可以节省交易的时间成本，另一方面，通过老客户的分享和推荐，有利于发展更多新客户。

8.4 Summary 小结

　　本章以出口业务为引导，展示并分析了10封信函，涵盖索赔和售后的各个环节。

　　1. 索赔与理赔

　　在国际贸易中，投诉和索赔是经常会出现的。发生损失后，受损方首先应搜集相关证据，然后根据合同或条款规定，找准相关责任人提出索赔。索赔函中应明确问题及损失情况，如品质问题、数量问题、交期问题、包装问题等，并提出具体索赔要求。

　　收到客户的索赔函后，需要及时处理。如果暂时不能回复或需要争取一定的时间思考和讨论，建议先发送一封回函告知客户：索赔信息收到，将尽快调查后回复（We got your claim message, will do the investigation and reply ASAP.）。然后等公司内部达成一致的处理意见后，再撰写理赔函予以回复。

处理索赔要慎重，首先要核实事实并查明原因，然后结合具体情况撰写理赔函。

遇到无理索赔时，要撰写拒绝赔付函给予回应。不是简单地拒绝，要明确说明不予赔偿的原因，拿出证据，据理力争，让对方明白事情的真相，并期望取得对方的理解。

如果确认是己方责任，不仅要在第一时间向客户道歉，还应具体问题具体分析，仔细研究并给出补救措施或解决方案。解决索赔的目的是要让双方减少彼此的损失，为未来的继续合作铺平道路。有些情况下，赔款并非解决索赔的最佳方式。要学会换位思考，站在客户的角度探索多种方式，比如：给客户重新补一批货，或者发一些别的产品，或者免费试销新品，等等。

2. 售后函

一笔生意的达成，从前期联络起步，经过开发信、询盘的处理、报价、交易细节谈判、确认订单和签约，直到合同履行和售后跟进，积极而有效的往来函电贯穿始终。

函电是商务谈判和彼此沟通的载体。但是，谈判与沟通并不等同，谈判只是沟通中的一部分，沟通是人与人之间的交流。保持沟通，着眼未来，与客户保持沟通和持续性跟进，是维系长期业务关系的有效手段。

售后函的作用就是跟进客户，目的是维系客户忠诚度，把客户培养成老客户。售后函的内容可以是询问销售情况，可以是新品或促销推介，也可以是售后咨询服务，还可以是简单的节日问候，等等。售后函的内容撰写和联络频率，要结合不同的客户和业务情况分别处理。

对于稳定的订单客户，建议每一到两个月联络一次，重点维护。对于偶尔下单客户，可以每三到五个月联络一次，以推荐新品和告知促销活动为主要沟通内容。跟进客户，沟通是贯穿始终的，要一直保持联系，一直跟进下去，这样生意才能长久。

8.5 Useful Words & Expressions 实用词汇及短语

1. claim

v. & n. 索赔，索款，索汇；提出要求

claim for 表示索赔原因或金额，claim后面也可直接跟索赔金额

claim on/against 表示对什么货物索赔

claim from/against/on/with 表示向某人索赔

claim 做名词，常与动词lodge, file, raise, make 等搭配使用。

lodge a claim against/with sb. for sth. 为某事向某人提出索赔

We have to claim $ 2,000 from you on this shipment for inferior quality. 由于质量问题，对于这批货物我方不得不向你方索赔2,000美元。

We shall lodge a claim against the insurance company for the goods damaged during transit. 对于货物在运输途中损坏，我方将向保险公司提出索赔。

We file a claim against you for the short delivery of 150 lbs. 我方向贵方提出短交 150 磅的索赔。

claim letter 索赔函

accept/admit/entertain/handle a claim 受理索赔

settle a claim 解决索赔

accept a claim 同意索赔

reject a claim 拒绝索赔

withdraw/waive a claim 放弃/驳回索赔

2. compensation

n. 赔偿, 补偿; 报酬

The buyer claimed a compensation for USD1,000 for the damage. 对于货物的损坏, 买方要求赔偿 1,000 美元。

We reserve the right to claim compensation from you for any damage. 我方将保留就损害向贵方要求索赔的权利。

compensation trade 补偿贸易

full compensation 全额赔偿

compensate

v. 赔偿; 补偿

compensate for 补偿

You should compensate us for the loss caused by the late delivery. 贵方必须向我方赔偿因迟交货物所引起 的损失。

complain

v. 抱怨; 申诉; 投诉

complaint

n. 抱怨; 控诉; 投诉

complain to sb. about/of sth. 向某人抱怨某事

make/have/report/a complaint with/against sb. on sth. 向某人抱怨某事

receive a complaint on sth. 收到关于某事的投诉

The most common complaint is about poor service. 最常见的投诉与服务差有关。

I'm going to complain to the manager about this. 我要就这件事向经理投诉。

3. replacement

n. 替代物; 代替或被替代的行为或过程; 替换

replace

v. 替换; 提供代替品

Please send the goods we need to replace those damaged during transit. 请立即寄来我们所需要的商品来代替在运输途中受损的商品。

4. at one's disposal 任某人处理（使用、支配等）

We put the business at the exclusive agent's disposal in Japan. 我们把在日本的业务交由那里的独家代理全权处理。

Shall we return them to you, or hold them at your disposal? 是退还给你们，还是留着听候你们处理？

5. presume

v. 认为；假定；推测

We presume that there must be some reasons for your having trouble with this article. 我们想，一定是有什么原因导致了该产品出了问题。

6. have no choice but to... 不得不/只能做某事

We have no choice but to cancel the order. 我们不得不取消订货。

We have no choice but to file a claim against you, which we hope will receive your prompt attention. 我们只能向贵方提出索赔，希望你们能马上关注此事。

7. be for one's account 由某人承担

8. consignment

n. 货物；运送的 货物；寄售；寄售的货物

9. on going into the matter 经调查此事

10. conclude

v. 完成

conclude our transaction 完成交易

同样的表述还有：fufill/finish the transaction

11. accordingly

adv. 相应地；照着办

12. unsalable

adj. 卖不掉的；无销路的

13. needless to say 不用说

14. inferior

adj.（质量等）差的，次的，劣等的

inferior quality 质量差

15. there is no ground for… 是毫无根据的，是站不住脚的

16. assume

v. 承担；担任

assume responsibility 承担责任

17. whatsoever

pron. 无论什么（意同whatever，但语气比whatever强）

18. barcode

n. 条形码

19. re-work

n. 二次加工；返工

20. recalled

v. 召回

21. patent issue 专利问题

22. distribution 分销，批发；分发

23. retail status 零售情况

24. 10-year-anniversary 十周年纪念

25. all-line products 全线产品

26. message online 在线消息

27. color difference 色差

28. short weight 短重

short shipped 短装

short calculated 少算

short paid 少付

29. late delivery 迟交

30. wrong delivery 错发

31. inspection fee/survey charge 检验费

相关表述：

inspection certificate of quality　品质检验证

inspection certificate of quantity　数量检验证

inspection certificate of weight　重量检验证

inspection certificate on damaged cargo　验残检验证

8.6 Useful Sentences 实用语句

1. After checking the goods against your invoice, we discovered a considerable shortage in number.

对照发票进行查验之后，我们发现数量少了很多。

2. On examing the goods received, we find that several items on the contract haven't been delivered. We enclose a list of the missing articles for your inspection.

验货之后我们发现合同中的好几种商品都没有到货。随函附上未到货的商品明细供您检验。

3. As the quality of the goods were much lower than required, we therefore are lodging a claim of $1,500 for inferior quality.

鉴于货物质量比要求低得多，我们要对低质量进行价值1500美元的索赔。

4. Upon the arrival of the last consignment in London, it was found, much to our regret, that about 60% of the cases were leaking.

上批货到达伦敦时，令我们非常遗憾的是，约有60%的箱子都有渗漏。

5. We have duly received the canned mushroom. However, the quality and packing method of the goods are nothing like those stipulated in contract.

我方已收到罐装蘑菇。然而，此批货物的质量和包装方式与双方在合同中规定的不一致。

6. As informed in previous letters, this lot of goods is of extremely inferior quality and our clients are unwilling to take them. We wonder if we should return or keep them in our warehouse at your disposal.

如前函所告，该批货物质量低劣，我方客户不愿提货，故请告知是否要我方将这批货退回或保存在仓库，留待你方处理。

7. The survey report issued by CCIB is forwarded and your early settlement is requested.

随附中国商品检验局的检验报告，希望你方早日理赔。

8. We must ask you to replace them with good salable ones.

我们必须请求贵方以适于销售的货物更换该货。

9. We hope that you will take your commercial reputation into consideration in all seriousness and open the L/C at once. Otherwise, you will be responsible for all the losses caused.

希望你方能认真考虑你们的商业信誉，立即开证，否则由此带来的损失由你方负担。

10. In order to compensate you for the trouble we are prepared to offer a special discount.

为了补偿我们给贵方带来的麻烦，我们准备给贵方特别的折扣。

11. As requested，we will send you a replacement within a week and hope you will be pleased with the new lot.

根据你们的要求，我们将在一周内更换货物，希望你们能对新一批的货物感到满意。

12. On thorough inspection, we find the goods were intact during packing. Thus, they were damaged due to rough handling.

我方全面检查，发现货物在装运时仍处于完好状态。 因此，货物损坏是由途中粗暴搬运导致。

13. Your payment is past due. Please deduct the claim USD 3,000 and settle the rest part to us ASAP.

你的付款已经延期了。请扣除索赔的3,000美元，尽早把剩余部分汇给我们。

14. These new products could be delivered in 3 days after package.

这些产品在包装后能在3日内发送。

15. Thank you for your great supports for our company's products over the past few years and I hope we will enjoy a better cooperation relation in the coming year.

对于您在过去的关照在此深表感谢，并且希望今后我们能一如既往地长期合作。

16. We currently are offering 20% discount of all-line products.

目前，我们全线产品有20%的优惠。

17. We have a promotion only for current customers this month, say a 10% discount.

我们本月仅针对老客户还有10%的优惠。

18. The company does after-sale service for us.

这个公司帮我们处理售后服务事宜。

19. I wish you'd reconsider to try our new and improved item.

但愿您能重新考虑一下我们更新换代的产品。

20. We're willing to go down the price if you could pay for the tooling cost.

如果你方支付模具费，我们愿意把产品的价格降下来。

8.7 Exercises 练习

I Translate the following words and expressions into English or Chinese.

1. 补偿贸易

2. 全线产品

3. 零售情况

4. 分销

5. 短装

Key8.1

6. settle a claim

7. inferior quality

8. barcode

9. packing list

10. inspection certificate of quality

II Choose the best answer.

1. We hope to do_____business with you in the near future.

A. the newly   B. fresh   C. novel   D. the latest

2. I would like to check _____you about the distribution and retail status.

A. up   B. on   C. with   D.to

3. Have you sold them _____?

A. on   B. out   C. all   D.in

4. We would like to express our deeply regret that the _____ for 10% goods couldn't be scanned.

A. packing   B. quality   C. passcode   D. barcode

5. It is too expensive _____do the re-work in UK.

A. to   B. at   C. in   D. with

6. If we had been informed in time, we _____ them for you.

    A. reserve   B. will serve   C. will have reserved   D. would have reserved

7. In accordance with our agreement, we have _____ at 30 days sight for the amount of the enclosed invoice.

    A. drawn on you   B. written to you   C. called on you   D. advised you

8. In order to promote business between us to our mutual advantage, we shall consider _____ your suggestions.

    A. accepting   B. accept   C. to accept   D. acceptance

9. As instructed, we will draw _____ you a sight draft for collection through the Bank of China.

    A. for   B. against   C. on   D. from

10. We have lodged a claim _____ the seller for the shortage of _____ S. S HAIHE.

    A. with, under   B. on, as per   C. with, to   D. against, ex

Ⅲ Translate the following sentences into English or Chinese.

    1. 兹附上一份检验报告作为我们索赔的依据。

    2. 您能否告知贵公司下一季的采购计划？

    3. 很遗憾，我们必须向你方投诉第233号订单货物的发货延迟。

    4. 我们正在调查这一事件，请贵方耐心等待，我们将反馈给贵方。

    5. 我方已经收到装运的3个订单项下的全部款项。

    6. We must therefore lodge a claim against you for the amount of USD 25,700.

    7. Regarding Order No. 228 , we have noticed a discrepancy in size and color from your original sample.

    8. I would like to check with you about the distribution and retail status of our products.

    9. Your claim cannot be accepted because it is lodged 30 days after the arrival of the goods at the destination.

    10. We have already written to you twice reminding you of the importance of prompt delivery, but as you have failed to make delivery on time you leave us with no choice but to cancel the order.

Ⅳ Translate the following body of the letter into English.

    我方已接到由"和平"轮于8月14日运抵的货物，承蒙贵公司及时发运订货，不胜感激。

    检验时，发现除第25号箱外皆完好无损，且符合订单所列要求。

    当打开第25号箱时，我方发现箱内货物并非我们订购的产品，相信是在装运货物时出了差错，箱内所装是其他订单的货物。

    因我方急需这些货物配齐整套系列产品销售，烦请及时安排发运替换产品，这些产品都列在附寄清单上。请核对我方订单和贵公司发票副本。

与此同时,我方将代为保管错运的货箱听候处理,请传真告知安排事宜。

V Writing task.

Read the following complaint letter and write a reply to it as per the business background and information.

对于这封投诉函,部门主管的回复是拒绝,不同意退货。

相关理由和解决方案:公司产品质量优良,广受认可,这次估计是个别检测疏忽导致的偶发事件。出问题的货物数量不多,可以替换一下被投诉的这些货品,然后考虑再给5个点的折扣。

请以公司业务员的身份,结合主管的意见和解决方案,撰写一封回函,尽量说服客户接受该解决方案。

Subject: Complaint for H-M Ear-phones under Order No.199

Dear Aria,

We have recently received a number of complaints from our customers about your H-M ear-phones, which apparently does not comply with the samples you sent us.

The H-M ear-phones complained about are about half of the 2,000 in the third wooden case under our Order No. 199. We ourselves examined some of the complained ones and found that they often don't make any sounds.

Therefore, we have to ask you to return the unsold balance of the goods, amounting to 48 pieces in all, and replace them with the goods of the same quality as the sample you sent us.

We look forward to your reply sooner.

Yours truly,

David

8.8 Supplement & Extension 补充与拓展

客户与礼物

一、该给谁送礼物呢?

1.长久合作的老客户

有些客户是非常稳定的老客户,合作几年且持续下单,这些客户应首先被归入送礼之列,同时也是重点维护对象。

2.潜力大的客户

有些客户刚开发不久,才合作过一两次,但根据产品和市场综合判断,具有长期合作的可能性。这样的客户可以尝试寄送礼物,通过礼物增进好感,为后续沟通建立良好的基础。

3.朋友一样的客户

有些客户在交易合作与交流过程中,联络沟通愉悦,变成了朋友,甚至对彼此的家庭也较为熟悉。这样的客户,也应寄送一份礼物。

二、如何选礼物?

1.礼物的挑选原则

首先要有中国特色,其次不宜太贵,同时还要注意不要太重、太大和太脆。商务沟通不是私人交往,商务礼品寄送一般是具有持续性的,不能今年寄,明年不寄。礼轻情意重,送的礼物太贵,一方面不好持久,另一方面也耗费金钱。礼物太重、太大或太脆,相应的快递运费就贵,且不好包装,在运输中容易损坏。

总之,实惠、轻便、有特色是商务礼物挑选的原则。

2.礼物分类

（1）男女客户通用的礼物:京剧玩偶、京剧剪纸画、京剧绢人、川剧变脸娃娃、刺绣杯垫、喜庆娃娃摆件、国风小泥人摆件、古风手绘记事笔记本、中国结、中国风设计小夜灯、玉如意U盘等。

（2）客户家人适合的礼物:传统娃娃虎头鞋、中国古典木质立体建筑模型、中国风风筝、原创民族风配饰系列（手链、项链、胸针等)、漆器彩绘置物盒、民族风围巾与小包、刺绣披肩等。

（3）适合男性客户的其他礼物:中国风鼻烟壶、景泰蓝烟灰缸、丝绸卷轴画、国风小屏风等。

实战系列案例一：

以退为进、适度引导、

突破低价、达成交易

9.1 问题的提出

在外贸业务中,价格对于成交非常重要。

在价格磋商环节,该如何突破客户的低价纠缠? 如何既可以提高报价,又能顺利达成交易?

9.2 业务背景与说明

这个系列案例,从卖方发出开发信,直到买方下订单,买卖双方围绕LED灯条的价格进行了数轮次的沟通,共12封邮件。

卖方:Monica—宁波一家主营LED灯具相关产品的工厂业务员

买方:Mike—伊朗的贸易商

01:8/20,Monica的开发信

Subject:Supply LED Lights

Dear Sir/Madam,

We are a professional LED lights manufacturer for 10 years and export to the USA, UK, France, Russia, Canada 600,000 pcs per year.

We are OEM supplier for Philips, Osram and help them raise their market share 18.5% in last 3 years.

Our catalogue is enclosed for your reference. We supply 1 year guarantee and all the products with CE & RoHS.

Any questions or inquiring, please contact me.

Yours truly,

Monica

正文译文1:

我们是一家拥有10年历史的专业LED灯具厂家,产品远销美、英、法、俄罗斯和加拿大等国,年销售量60万只。

我们是菲利普、欧司朗的贴牌合作伙伴,在过去的3年里已经帮助他们提升了18.5%的市场份额。

随函附上目录供参考。我们的产品有1年的质保期,所有产品均通过CE和RoHs认证。

如有任何问题，请联系我。

02：8/28，Mike 的询盘信

Subject：Inquiry for LED Strips

Hi,

We import LED strips and LED bulbs from China.

Please send us your offer on LED strips, Model：NW-2835-SMD 60.

We sell around 20 km LED strips and around 2,000 pcs bulbs a month at present.

Regards,

Mike

正文译文2：

我们从中国进口LED灯条和LED球灯泡。

请发送型号为NW-2835-SMD 60的LED灯条报价。

我们目前月销大约20千米的灯条和2,000只球灯泡。

情景分析：

从七月初开始至今，Monica已经发送了近百封开发信，却始终没有得到回复。8月28日，Monica收到了这封询盘。从客户的询盘中，Monica初步判断这个客户有一定的质量，每年的销量也不算少。于是Monica决定先给客户报价，看看客户的反应。

03：9/1，Monica 的发盘信

Subject：Quote Sheet for Led Strips

Hi Mike,

Thank you for your reply.

The attachment is our quotation, please check it.

Regards,

Monica

Encl：Quotation sheet for LED strips.

正文译文3：

感谢您的回复。

附件是报价单，请查收。

04：9/5，Mike的还价函

Subject：Reply to Quote Sheet for Led Strips

Dear Monica,

I checked your price list, and we will not make any deal in this price.

I give your prices which I actually pay: USD 1.40/m.

Regards,

Mike

正文译文4：

我查看了您发送的报价单，我们不能接受以这个价格成交。

我给出的价格是每米1.4美元。

情景分析：

在Monica报价后，客户认为价格太高了，同时给出了自己的目标价。而客户这个目标价和原报价相差较大，甚至比成本价还要低0.05美元。

这种情况是业务员报价后经常会遇到的问题。对于这种目标明确或者说是还价还得很过分的客户，需要根据具体情况分别处理。有一个可供参考的建议是：冷处理。

具体做法是：在收到客户的还价信后，不要立即回复。即便这个还价是我们能够接受的，也不要立即答应客户的要求，而是先搁置一段时间不予回复，比如1~3周。可以利用这段时间判断一下这个客户是否是真正的买家，同时也向客户暗示公司目前订单充足，不急于低价接单。

在这个冷处理期，会有两种情况发生：一是客户着急了，发来邮件催问情况；另一种是客户也很淡然，这中间也不主动联系卖家。这个案例是后者，Monica一直拖延着不回复，客户也并没有催问，就这样过了20多天。9月26日，Monica撰写了一封回复函。

05：9/26，Monica对Mike还盘的回复

Subject：Led Strips Pricing

Dear Mike,

I have negotiated with my manager about your case.

We can do products according to your price USD 1.40/pc.

Free samples can be sent to you for your reference.

Regards,

Monica

正文译文5：

　　我已经和我们经理沟通过你的这单生意。

　　我们可以按照您的目标价格每米1.4美元供货。

　　免费样品可以提供给您测试。

情景分析：

　　Monica在这个对买方还盘的回复函中，既没有解释为什么延迟了20多天才回复，也没有进行再还价，而是直接就接受了客户还盘中提出的目标价格。同时还表示，可以提供免费的样品以供质量测试。

　　如果你是客户，在还了一个较低的价格后就一直没收到卖方的任何消息，而20多天之后，突然收到这样一封卖家的回复信，不仅全盘接受了你的还价，同时还主动提出可提供免费样品。那么，你也应该是比较惊喜的吧？

　　客户当天下午就回复了一封很长的邮件给Monica，详述了对产品的质量要求，同时催促Monica发送样品。

06：9/26，Mike催促发样品

Subject：Led Strips Samples

Dear Monica,

Thank you for your reply. We appreciated that you offered me such attractive prices.

Anyway, price is no problem. We expect stable quality and there are few factors.

1. LEDs must have constant CCT so there cannot be any difference in colour between particular LEDs, we always check through milky acrylic sheet.

2. There cannot be any dead LEDs or cold solders.

3. PCB must be at least 0.25 mm thickness and has white solder mask.

If any of point happened then we can't accept goods.

Anyway, please send us samples at first. After we confirm, we send them to our quality control company. They will compare samples with produced goods before each delivery.

If you agree for these terms, we need samples of your strips（1 m each color）, and then we can start cooperation.

Regards,

Mike

正文译文6：

感谢回复。我们很满意您提供给我如此有吸引力的价格。

现在价格已经不是问题。我们希望产品有稳定的质量，且符合以下要求。

1. 发光二极管必须有稳定的色温，二极管之间的色彩不能有任何色差，我们一直是通过乳白色亚克力表进行测试。

2. 不能有任何死角LED或冷焊。

3. 线路板必须在0.25毫米厚，同时用白色阻焊。

如果以上任何一点不能达标，我们就不能接受您的产品。

首先，请发样品给我们。我们确认后，会送往我们的质量控制中心。他们将在每次交货时将样品与大货做比较检测。

如果同意以上条件，我们需要灯条样品每种颜色一米，这样我们才能够开始交易合作。

07：9/28，Monica 对催样函的回复

Subject：Led Strips Samples

Dear Mike,

We will arrange samples as soon as possible.

Regards,

Monica

正文译文 7：

我们将尽快给您安排样品。

情景分析：

低价对于客户是很有吸引力的。只要价格符合客户的心理预期，不要说20多天，就是再久不联系，客户也不会忘记你的。

卖方同意了客户超低价格的还盘，同时也回复了将尽快提供样品。但是之后，就再次沉默了。这中间双方没有任何消息往来，既没有给客户寄送样品，也没有其他沟通。

半个月后，客户等不及了，于是在10月14日发来了再次催促样品的催样函。

08：10/14, Mike第二次催发样品

Subject：Led Strips Samples Again

Hi Monica,

Long time no reply from you.

I am waiting for your samples, as I have to place an order with around 20 km strips. I have to be sure it will be good quality and meet my requirements.

For this order I must get goods before 10th December. So I need samples of LED strips very quickly.

Please reply me asap.

Regards,

Mike

正文译文 8：

很久没收到你的回复。

我一直在等您的样品，以便安排20千米灯条的订单。我需要确认你的产品是否符合我们的质量要求。

这次的订单，我需要在12月10日拿到货。因此，我需要尽快拿到样品。

盼速复。

09：10/15，Monica的回复函

Subject：Led Strips

Dear Mike,

Thank you for your E-mail of October 14. I am sorry for the late reply.

We can offer you the best price USD 1.4, but the quality will not be good. Our price for NW-2835-SMD 60 is USD 1.8, we sell it well in European market. We guarantee one year quality. It means that if it doesn't work with one year, we will send you new one.

But if we offer USD 1.4 , we have to use bad material to replace it. If we send this goods to you, we can make money, but you will meet many problems from your clients.

We can not do this business in this way, we will never make fast dollar. I am so sorry about that, we have to cancel this case. We really want to establish a long term cooperation with you, but we can't provide you bad quality.

Sorry for bringing troubles to you.

Monica

正文译文9：

感谢你10月14日的邮件。很抱歉回复您晚了。

我可以给您的最好价格是1.4美元，但质量不会很好。我们NW-2835-SMD 60的价格是1.8美元，这个是在欧洲热卖的。我们的保质期是一年。这意味着它们在一年内如果出现任何问题，我们将给您发新的产品。

但是如果我们按1.4美元来供货，我们就必须用差的原料来生产。如果我们发送那样的货给您，我们虽然是赚钱了，但是您将面对客户的许多责问。

我们不做"一锤子"买卖，那不是我们的生意原则。很抱歉，我们不得不取消这个订单。我们是准备与您长期合作的，但是我们确实不能给您提供次品。

抱歉给您带来的困扰。

情景分析：

在收到客户关于样品的第二封催促函后，Monica很快就给客户发送了一封长信。表达了为了长期合作而拒绝提供次品的做法，强调宁可不接单也不愿损失信誉。

实际上，LED灯条这个产品，卖家的销售价是每米1.8美元，成本价格是1.45美元左右，

而客户的目标价是1.4美元。从一开始，这个还价就已经将生意的大门关闭了。

针对这种情况，卖家采用了冷处理和以退为进的策略。在双方沟通到第9封信的时候，把球抛给了客户，让客户自己去做决定。

客户收到这个邮件的具体心态，无从推测。但是3日后，客户发回了一封篇幅较长的邮件，标题用了Final Price（最终价格）这样的字眼。

10：10/18, Mike 的回复函

Subject：Final Price for Led Strips

Dear Monica,

I am glad that you are honest with me. I know that some China manufacturers use bad quality materials to achieve as low as possible price.

Personally I want to buy better quality goods. But price pressure on my market compels me to find the cheapest offers. So we can pay up to USD 1.60/m if it will be your regular good quality product.

Please consider it. I decided to pay more just for quality, but if it will be more expensive then it is not profitable for me.

For considering cooperation, I have to get samples for exactly goods which you want to provide me in future suppliers.

If you agree for it, pls prepare samples for me asap.

Regards,

Mike

正文译文 10：

很高兴您对我的真诚。我知道一些中国厂家为了达到尽可能低的价格，用差的原料生产。

从我个人来说，我想采购高质量的产品。但是我这边的市场压力很大，迫使我需要找到最便宜的供货商。因此，如果您的产品质量达标，我们可以提升采购价格到1.6美元/米。

请考虑我的意见。我可以为提升质量多加点钱，但是如果价格太高，我们也是无法接受的。

为了我们的合作，如果您想成为我们的供货商，我必须拿到样品。

如果同意，请尽快准备样品给我。

11: 10/19, Monica的寄样函

Subject: Led Strips Samples

Hi Mike,

Samples have been sent to you today. Maybe you can get them in 10 days.

Regards,

Monica

正文译文11:

样品已于今天寄送。预计您将在10天内收到。

12: 10/30, Mike的订单函

Subject: Order for Led Strips

Dear Monica,

Your samples have been received and I have to say that I am glad of their quality.

If you promise to keep same quality all time, we can start our cooperation.

The attachment is our order, pls check it.

Regards,

Mike

正文译文12:

样品已经收到, 对它们的质量我很满意。

如果你保证品质如一, 我们可以开始合作了。

附件是我们的订单, 请查收。

情景分析:

最终, Monica和客户以1.6美元的价格成交了。Monica的初始报价是1.8美元, 客户的初始还价是1.4美元, 经过数轮沟通, 双方各自退让了一步, 最终达成了交易。

9.3 案例总结

报价与还价，说到底还是沟通，而沟通是一门艺术。

在这个案例中，Monica在发出近百封开发信后，终于收到了一个客户的询盘。但是，报价后就被客户直接还了一个超低的目标价，根本无法成交。在这种情况下，Monica并未急于跟客户就价格进行再次沟通，而是基于对行业产品质量和价格的了解，采取了冷处理和以退为进的策略。

首先对于客户的还价函冷处理：保持沉默，不予回复，等待客户的反应。在外贸业务中，通常客户在还价后，会等待卖方的反馈，而很少主动跟进自己的还价。在这个案例中，也是如此。三周过去了，双方没有任何联络。

三周后，估计客户已经对自己的这个还价不抱希望的时候，却突然收到Monica的回函。回函中未做任何解释，只是表示接受客户当初的还价，并主动提出可以寄送免费样品。

低价对于客户的吸引力是毋庸置疑的。尽管三周没有任何音讯，但是在接到了Monica的这封回函后，客户马上做出了回应。当天下午就发送回复函给Monica，详述了对产品的质量要求，同时希望尽快发送相关样品。

对于客户的这个回函，Monica的反应也很迅速。收信后不到两天就回复了一封短函，答应客户寄送样品。但实际并未付诸行动，而是再次进入沉默状态，以待时机。

那边，客户一直在等样品，可是一直没有消息。整整两周，既没有寄送样品，也没有做任何解释。这时候，客户坐不住了。对于这个价格他是很满意的，同时还有交货期临近的压力。于是，在收到Monica这封答应寄送样品的回函半个月后，客户给Monica发了一封催促寄送样品的函电，并提到了订单安排和交货期。

见到这封信函，Monica知道时机到了。于是，第二天就回复了客户一封言辞恳切的信函。明确表示，因价格问题，不得不取消订单，宁可不接单也不能提供次品给客户，并对客户表示歉意。

如果在客户初次还价并提出自己的目标价格时，Monica就明确表示这个价格做不下来，那么这个生意估计那会儿就画上句号了。但在此刻，经过了一系列的操作和沟通后，客户虽有不满，但也不会轻易放弃。

这个实战案例中，在收到这个邮件后，客户也很诚恳地回复了Monica一封邮件，主动提高了采购价格，并再次提到样品问题。而Monica也积极配合，在样品被确认后，最终以双方各让一步的价格达成交易。

小结：

当客户还价过低的时候，不可盲目接单或者直接拒绝。要以退为进，适度地引导，既要坚持底线，也要学会变通。

具体操作建议：

1. 先冷处理，暂不回复，等待客户的反应。

2. 在2~3周后，可以做出适当让步，将客户拉回或者吸住。

3. 以高品质引导客户回归正常的价格轨道。

4. 做好后续服务，让客户满意。

实战系列案例二：

关注高端、有效沟通、
循序渐进、高价成交

10.1 问题的提出

收到客户的询盘,必须尽快报价吗?

业务沟通中,只能程序化地询盘、报价、还价吗?

怎样才能获取更多信息? 如何才能发现并抓住高端客户?

怎样才能脱离价格血拼的死循环把利润做大?

10.2 业务背景与说明

这个系列案例,从买方发出询盘信,直到交易确定,买卖双方围绕价格和其他交易条件进行了数轮次的沟通,共13封邮件。

卖方: Monica——河南一家经营假发产品的贸易公司业务员

买方: Peter——英国的零售商

01: 客户的第一次询盘

Subject: Inquiry for Human Hair

Dear Monica,

Kindly forward me the price for 100 grams Remy human hair top quality you have.

Regards,

Peter

正文译文1:

请给我发100克顶级真人顺发的报价。

关于产品的注解:

grams,是计量单位克。Remy human hair 指的是真人顺发。

Remy hair是顺发的意思,就是真人的头发经过了处理,头发的毛鳞片都已经处理掉了,这样头尾颠倒了也不会打结,便于梳理。

02: Monica的回复函

Subject: Reply on Human Hair

Dear Peter,

Thanks for your interest for our products.

We could supply Indian Remy hair or Chinese Remy hair. Which kind of remy hair you are prefer?

I confirm that in this industry there are many grades of hair for different market need. But for your saying the "top quality", could you give me more descriptions about what kind of quality you want?

Waiting for your soon reply. Thank you.

Regards,

Monica

正文译文2：

谢谢您对我们的产品感兴趣。

我们可以提供印第安人真人顺发或华人真人顺发。您更喜欢哪种真人顺发？

在这个行业，我确信不同级别的假发会适用于不同地区的市场。由于您说需要顶级品质，您可以描述一下您需要什么级别的品质吗？

盼速复，谢谢。

情景分析：

客户的询价信，措辞非常简单，但是其中透露出对质量要求比较高的信息。这种情况下，直接报价并不可取。一方面，客户的询价条件不明确，不够清晰，难以直接匹配产品；另一方面，以什么样的价格水平报价，就现有的信息难以决定。

Monica在收到客户的询价函后，并没回复报价，而是提出了一些问题，以便获取更多的信息。一来试探客户的询价诚意，二来试探客户价格接受的范围。

03：客户的回复

Subject：Human Hair

Dear Monica，

Thanks for your reply. We are a retailer for hair extensions and cosmetics in London for more than a decade. We want to launch our own Remy human hair. We are selling Sensationnel, Milkyway, Freetress Sleek etc. at present.

Due to tough competition in this industry, profit margin has fallen very low and we want to cut middle men, hair brands. The aim is to introduce our remy hair in our 2 stores in the beginning and then introduce more variety of human hair.

I have contacted many companies in China and they sent me few samples, but unfortunately, none of them could match our quality. I sent them many hair samples which we are already using in our stores, but they could not make a same quality hair.

We want a quality same as Sensationnel's Remy goddess （if you know already） and if you ask me to send you some samples, then I will say that I am now fed up with those samples to many hair manufacturers which cost me nearly $700 until now.

At first we want a little quantity order and if we found this practice good. Then we will move into wholesale and whoever our manufacturer will be, obviously our turn over will generate more business for you.

We need a remy hair, a top quality hair which makes us a different so we could recognized in the crowed. Monica, a best hair means a best top quality human hair, what else can I describe? The texture should be verified by fire and not very silky.

Will wait for your reply.

Peter

正文译文3：

　　谢谢您的回复。我们是一家在伦敦有10年历史的假发产品和化妆品的零售商。我们想发展我们自己的真人顺发。我们目前在销售几个品牌的产品，比如 Sensationnel, Milkyway, Freetress Sleek等。

　　由于业内激烈的竞争，现在的产品利润很低，所以我们想跳过中间商、品牌商。目的是在我们自己的两家店里推广我们自己的真人顺发和其他更多的产品。

　　我联系了中国的很多公司，他们也给我发了一些样品，很不幸，没有一家可以达到我们的品质要求。我给他们发了许多在我们店卖的假发样品，但没有一家可以做到同样的品质。

　　我们需要和 Sensationnel品牌的雷米女神一样的品质（如果您听说过）。如果您需要，我可以给您发一些样品，我不得不说一下，到目前为止我发这些样品给许多厂家已经花费了我将近700美元了。

　　首先我会给你一个小量订单，如果我们对品质满意，我们将会批量订货和开展其他合作，当然在我们生意好转的时候会给你带来更多的生意。

　　我们需要真人顺发，与众不同的顶级品质才能确保我们能脱颖而出。Monica，最好的假发意味着顶级的真人发，我还有什么可说的呢？质地需要经过火烧验证，不能太柔滑。

盼复。

情景分析：

在收到Monica的回复后，客户发来了一封篇幅很长的函电，描述了公司情况和销售机会，表达了对质量的诉求，同时流露出目前没有合适供应商的问题，等等。

基于这些信息反馈，Monica觉得在价格方面，利润尺度是可以适当放大些的。那么，该如何让客户接受并认可产品的高价呢？

假发产品由于其小众化和非标准化，具有一定的价格优势。但是，同业竞争和价格对比也还是难以避免的。让客户自然地接受并认同产品的高质高价，是需要沟通技巧的。

04: Monica的回复函

Subject：Human Hair

Dear Peter,

Thanks for your kind mail. In this industry the hair has many grades for different markets' need. For some developing countries we mainly offer non-remy or synthetic products because it's what they can afford.

For the Remy hair, it's getting more and more precious, because now the girls go to dye their own hair, curl the hair or straighten them, so the top quality remy hair is more and more precious. That's why the price of the hair is getting more and more high and it's getting more and more popular in the market. We have been work with Sensational before. We know what you mean the top quality.

You know price is attached with the quality. We have a saying that in this industry, any price is OK for any products. The material is the factor. If you want the top quality hair extension, we could offer but here I want to notice you that the price would be a bit higher.

For small quantity order, we could work with you to do that. But if you have your own pack, you need to afford the extra cost as we need to customize small quantity for you. So please advise, what's the product you want, the style, weight, length, color and quantity. I could actual cost and quote our best price for you.

Waiting for your soon reply.

Regards,

Monica

正文译文4：

谢谢您的邮件。业内不同级别品质的假发都是针对不同地区的市场开发的。对于发展中国家，我们主要提供非雷米或合成材料的产品，因为他们只能接受这个。

关于真人顺发，它越来越珍贵，因为现在女孩们都染发、烫发或者拉直发，所以顶级真人顺发越来越稀缺。这也是市场上真人顺发的价格越来越高和越来越受欢迎的原因。我们之前和Sensationnel合作过。我们理解您的顶级品质的要求。

您知道价格和品质是直接挂钩的。我们直言在业内任何产品只要价格到位，产品就可以做。关键是原料的问题。如果您需要顶级品质的假发产品，我们可以提供，但我想提醒您价格将会比较高。

对于少量试单，我可以给您做。但如果您需要自己的包装，您需要额外加钱，因为我们需要为您少量定制。因此请告诉我，您需要什么样的产品，款式、重量、长度、颜色和数量，这些便于我给您计算成本并给您报我们最好的价格。

盼复。

情景分析：

Monica在给客户回复的时候，首先对行业内的产品情况和销售情况做了初步说明，唤起客户的认知；接着进一步解释了客户需要的产品的原料稀缺的原因，给客户展示出自己对市场的了解和专业性；同时指出公司和行业内知名品牌有过合作，因此十分理解客户对品质的细节要求，对客户对品质的要求表示认同，进一步拉近了和客户的距离。

这些说明和解释，让客户感觉到自己是在和一个资深内行人士进行沟通。接下来，在抛出产品价格会比较高的铺垫之后，让客户告知需要订货的产品的具体内容。一步一步，引导客户进入高质高价的轨道圈。

这封信发出后，客户回函说明了自己需要的产品详细规格，进行二次询价。

05: Peter的二次询盘信

Subject: Inquiry

Dear Monica，

I want to start with Remy goddess quality (if you have seen already). Kindly quote me the price for per 110 grams and each color, and I will be able to order you 10 packs per color. I will be ordering for 10, 12, 14, 18 inches in col 1, IB, 2, 4.

This would be a test order and please note as I mentioned in my email earlier that realistically I want to start a distribution in near future and we have to work together.

Quality, yes and price of course I am aware about it.

Waiting for your reply.

Peter

正文译文5：

如果您一切准备妥当，我想开始定一些雷米女神级假发。请给我报如下要求的产品价格：每色110克，我需要每色10包。我将订购10英寸、12英寸、14英寸、18英寸的列1、1B、2、4。

这个是试单，请看我之前邮件提到的部分。在近期我们确实想开始推广我们的产品了，我们将一起合作。

高质量是必须的，当然价格问题我也很关心。

盼复。

06：Monica的报价信

Subject: Quotation Sheet

Hi Peter,

Good morning. I'm really glad that you could place a trial order.

For the Remy goddess hair, we could supply the best Indian Remy hair, and the price pls see the attachment.

If it's OK, pls confirm the quantity to me.

I'll make a proforma invoice for your confirmation. Thank you.

Regards,

Monica

正文译文6：

早上好。很高兴您给我们下一个试订单。

对于女神级真人顺发，我们提供最好的印第安真人顺发，价格表见附件。

如果价格可以，请向我确认下数量。

收到您的确认后，我将给您做形式发票。

情景分析：

　　通过之前的多番铺垫，面对客户的第二次询盘，Monica直接报价了。这个时候，优质优价的逻辑已经成立了，此刻报价有利于订单水到渠成，避免了客户不断砍价的问题。

　　客户收到报价后，表示接受价格，并开始咨询样品问题。

07：客户询问样品

Subject：Sample

Dear Monica，

I am happy with the prices if its same quality as Remy goddess by Sensationnel.

Could you kindly send me a pack of 10 inch as a sample? Tell me the cost include DHL charges for that sample pack. Also tell me how I can pay you.

As soon as we receive sample and if the quality is what we are expecting. Then by all mean it will be fine to start a business with you.

Regards,

Peter

正文译文7：

　　如果质量和Sensationnel女神级真人顺发一样，我乐于接受您的价格。

　　您可以给我发一包10英寸的样品吗？请告诉我包含运费的价格。并告知我如何付款给您。

　　我们希望尽快收到质量达到我们预期的样品。然后我们就会开始良好的合作。

08：Monica的回复

Subject：Reply to Sample

Last year we did 2 orders for goddess. One is Indian Remy hair, the other one is Chinese Remy hair.

For the Chinese Remy hair, actually it's the top quality type in this industry because it's stronger than Indian human hair, and not easily to be broken. Of course the price is the most expensive.

I don't know whether they would be interesting to you.

For the payment, we could accept these 3 kinds:

1. Bank money transfer;

2. Western union;

3. Money gram.

Please advise your delivery address so I could check the freight for DHL.

Regards,

Monica

正文译文8：

去年我们做了2个女神级假发的订单。一个就是印第安真人顺发，另一个是华人真人顺发。

关于华人真人顺发，确实是业内的顶级品质的款式，因为它比印第安真人顺发韧性要强，不易损坏。当然价格也会更高。

我不知您是否对它们十分感兴趣。

关于付款方式，我们接受如下三种方式:1. 银行转账; 2. 西联汇款; 3. 速汇金。

请告诉我您的收货地址，以便我为您查询DHL运费。

情景分析：

在客户提出需要样品的时候，距离订单就又近了一步。在回复的时候，Monica并不是仅仅做了关于样品的回复，而是自然地介绍公司情况，并提到了另一个产品系列。

因为，从之前的沟通中，Monica了解到，客户是一个采购商，而采购商往往是能够被激发询问产品的同类或关联需求的。

果然，收到上述回函后，客户又发来一个询盘，提出对另一种材料的采购意愿。

09：Peter的又一个询盘

Subject: Inquiry

Dear Monica,

Good to know that at least I am talking to the person who knows what to do. Are you able to tell me if you can manufacture Chinese Remy hair and if you can then tell what the price will be. Please note I am not wasting your time and genuinely want to start my own brand.

I hope you will understand.

Peter

正文译文 9:
　　很高兴我在和一个内行人沟通。您能告诉我您是否可以用华人真人顺发生产,如果可以做,请告诉我价格。希望我没有浪费您的时间,我们真正想开始推广我们自己的品牌。
　　我希望您会理解。

情景分析:
　　Peter是一个采购商。作为采购商,客户都喜欢和内行人沟通,因为内行才容易了解客户的心理要求,客户在可以接受的价格范围内,通常是愿意多出点价钱向内行人订货的。
　　在收到这封信后,Monica着重分析了客户大概可以接受的价格,尺度已有把握,于是继续按那个高品质水准进行报价。

10: Monica的又一个报价函

Subject: Quotation for Chinese Remy Human Hair
Dear Peter,

The price for Chinese Remy human hair is attached.

Those hairs are the best quality in this industry. They are the thickest and the strongest, and all the cuticles are at the same direction.

If you more think about the quality, it would be your best choice.

Monica

正文译文 10:
　　华人真人顺发的价格请看附件。
　　这些是业内最好品质的假发,它们的厚度、韧性和所有的角质层是在同一方向上。
　　如果你更多地关注产品的品质,它就是您的最佳选择。

情景分析:
　　客户对这个报价很满意,没有还价,直接回复了下面的信函。

11：客户回复报价

Subject：Sample for Chinese Remy Human Hair

Dear Monica，

I am happy with the prices. Kindly forward me the total cost for 1 pack 10" Chinese Remy sample. I send you money so you can send the sample pack. Once we checked the sample, then we will place the regular orders.

Also, can you help us with design and packaging?

Regards,

Peter

正文译文11：

我很满意您的报价。请给我1包10英寸华人真人顺发的样品的所有费用。我给您付款后，您给我发样品。一旦我们确认了样品，我们将给您下正式的订单。

另外，您可以帮我们设计包装吗？

情景分析：

Monica要开始准备样品了。同时，还需要跟客户最后确定一些具体事宜。

12：Monica的业务沟通信

Subject：Other Details

Dear Peter，

I'm happy for your soon confirmation. Please advise me these info.

Which style you want?

Offer me your delivery address so I could check the freight to you.

Which kind of payment you prefer?

For the packaging, you could send the picture you want to print on the package, we could help you to do the post process to make sure the package is suitable for production.

Regards,

Monica

正文译文 12：

很高兴您的快速确认，请确认以下信息：

您需要什么款式？

请给我发您的收货地址，以便我给您查询运费。

您喜欢用哪种付款方式？

关于包装，请发一些您需要印刷到包装袋上的图案给我，我们在生产中会为您制作合适的包装。

13：Peter的回复信

Dear Monica，

Your reply is well noted.

I am leaving the office now and will send you all the information include my design within few hours.

Peter

正文译文 13：

已经收到您的回复。

我现在不在办公室，数小时内我将给您发包括我的设计在内的所有信息。

情景分析：

在这之后，客户Peter对于产品的质量很满意，开始了与Monica公司的长期合作。

10.3 案例总结

关注高端客户，是脱离低价纠缠的一个途径。但是如何发现高端客户，如何跟高端客户进行有效沟通，进而达成交易呢？这个案例提供了一个思路。

首先，在收到客户的询盘后，尤其是定位不够清晰明确的询价函时，先不要急于报价，但是要及时回复。在回复中，可以设计几个问题，唤起客户的兴趣，让客户主动讲出有价值的信息。

这个案例中，客户的第一封询盘是非常简短的，没有任何感情色彩。但是在Monica的回函后，客户的话匣子被打开了。

基于客户的信息反馈，可以初步判断出客户对于质量的关注度极高，归属高端客户之列。但这个时候，贸然报一个高价，难免还是会陷入讨价还价的价格旋涡，费时耗力，且结果未知。

在报价前，进行适度的铺垫，以专家的姿态介绍行业和产品信息，用替客户着想的热情态度去引导客户下单。由浅入深，逐步让客户做好价格高的心理预期和准备。然后，再结合客户对于样品的要求情况，报出相对合理的高价位。

事实上，高端客户为了维护自身产品品牌，会挑选更为专业的供应商进行合作，即使价格高一些也会接受。在商务沟通中，成功树立起专家形象的业务员与客户讨论的重点更多是品质和设计，从而避免进入血拼价格的死循环。

小结：

在外贸销售中，了解客户的关注点，非常重要。要投其所好，深入分析客户看重质量，还是价格，或者是交货期等，要区别对待。

收到询盘后，先不要急于按常规回复报价。可以结合询盘内容，设计几个问题来探查客户的真实想法，尤其是一些非标准化或小众产品。然后，结合客户的关注点，寻找机会。

对于质量尤为关注的客户，可以大致归为高端客户。高端客户会优选更为专业或具有服务特色的供应商合作，而不会过于专注低价，毕竟高质高价是常理。

关注高端客户是脱离血拼价格的一个途径，但是要让高端客户认可并保持愉快沟通，外贸业务员就必须打造业内专家的形象。作为外贸业务员，不断提升自身的行业专业知识是能接到高利润订单的有利因素。而培养和留住专家型外贸业务员，是企业开拓国际高端产品市场的有效路径。

Appendix

附录：外贸英语常用缩略词语表

A

A/C	account 账户
A. M.	ante meridiem 上午
Art.	article 条款；货物；项
ASAP	as soon as possible 尽快
ATTN	attention 经办人，注意
A. R.	All Risks 一切险
AWB	air waybill 空运提单

B

Bal	balance 差额
Bar.	barrel 桶；琵琶桶
B. clause	both to blame collision clause 船舶互撞条款
B/B	breakbulk 散件杂货
B/G	bonded goods 保税货物
B/L	bill of lading 提单

C

C. A. D.；C/D	cash against documents 付现交单
CAF	currency adjustment factor 货币贬值附加费
C. B. D.	cash before delivery 先付款后交单
CBM	cubic metre 立方米
C. C.	chamber of commerce 商会
C. C. I. B	China Commodity Inspection Bureau 中国商品检验局
CFR	cost and freight 成本加运费
CFS	container freight station 集装箱集散站；集装箱货运站
CIC	china insurance clauses 中国保险条款
CIF	cost, insurance and freight 成本费、运费加保险费
CIP	carriage and insurance paid to 运费和保险费付至

CLP	container load plan 集装箱/装载计划表
Co.	company 公司
C/O	certificate of origin 原产地证明书
C. O. C.	carrier's own container 船主提供集装箱
C. O. D.	cash on deliver 交货付现
Corp.	corporation 公司
COSCO	China Ocean Shipping Company 中国远洋运输公司
CPT	carriage paid to 指定运费付至
CTN	carton 纸箱
C. W. O.	cash with order 订货时付款；现金订货
CY	container yard 集装箱堆场

D

D/A	document against acceptance 承兑交单
DAF	delivered at frontier 货交边境
D/D	demand draft 票汇
DDC	destination delivery charge 目的地提货费
DDP	delivered duty paid 赋税后交货
DDU	delivered duty unpaid 未完税交货
DES	delivered ex-ship 船上交货
DEQ	delivered ex-quay 仓库交货
D. C.	dangerous goods 危险品货物
D/O	delivery order 提货单；交货单
D/P	document against payment 付款交单
DPP	damage protection plan 集装箱损坏保险

E

EDI	electronic date interchange 电子数据交换
E. & O. E.	errors & omissions excepted 有错当查
Enc.; Encl.	enclosure 附件
ETA	estimated time of arrival 预计到达时间
ETD	estimated time of departure 预计离开时间
EXW	ex-works 工厂交货

F

| FAK | freight all kinds 同一费率 |
| F. A. Q. | fair average quality 大路货；中等品质 |

FAS	freight alongside ship（装运港）船边交货
FCA	free carrier 货交承运人
FCL	full container load 集装箱整箱货
FCR	forwarder's cargo receipt 承运人领货单
F. I.	free in 船方不负责装船费用
F. I. O	free in and out 船方不负担装卸费
FIOST	free in. out, stowed & trimmed 船方不负担装船、卸船、理仓及平仓费用
F. O.	free out 船方不负责卸船费用
FOB	free on board 离岸价格
F. O. R.	free on rail 火车上交货
F. O. T.	free on truck 货车上交货
F. P. A.	free from particular average 平安险
F/R	flat rack container 平板集装箱

G

GATT	General Agreement on Tariffs and Trade 关税贸易总协定
G. M. Q	good merchantable quality 尚好可销品质
GSP	generalized system of preferences 普惠制
GW	gross weight 毛重

H

HAWB	house Air Waybill 空运代理行提单
H/H	half Height Container 半高集装箱
HS	Harmonized Commodity Description and Coding System 商品名称及编码协调制度

I

IATA	International Air Transport Organization 国际民航运输协会
ICC	International Chamber of Commerce 国际商会
ICC	Institute Cargo Clause 英国伦敦协会货物保险条款
IMO	International Maritime Organization 国际海事组织
IMF	International Monetary Fund 国际货币基金组织
Inc.	incorporated 股份有限公司
Incoterms	International Rules for the Interpretation of Trade Terms 国际贸易术语解释通则
ISO	International Standard Organization 国际标准化组织

K

KG.	kilogram 公斤；千克

L

LASH	lighter aboard ship 载驳船
L/C	letter of gredit 信用证
LCL	less（than）container load 集装箱拼箱货
L/G	letter of guarantee 保函
L. I. O.	liner in and out 船方负责装卸费，但不包括码头费
L. O. A.	length overall 全长
Ltd.	limited 有限公司

M

Max.	maximum 最大额
Memo.	memorandum 备忘录
Min.	minimum 最小额
MNC	multi-national corporation 跨国公司
M/R	mate's receipt 大幅收据；收货单
MT	matric ton 公吨
M/T	mail transfer 信汇
V.	motor vessel 轮船

N

NO.	number 号数
N. O. E.	not otherwise enumerated 除非另行列明
N. O. S.	not otherwise specifed 除非另有指定
NTBs	non-tariffs barriers 非关税壁垒
N. W.	net weight 净重
NWC	net working capital 净流动资本
N/P	net profit 净利

O

O/A	open account 赊销
O. C. P.	Overland Common Point 水陆联运转换点
O/H	over height 超出正常高度
O. P.	open policy 预约保单

O/S	open side container 开边集装箱
O/T	open top container 开顶集装箱
O/W	over width 超出正常宽度

P

PC.	piece 件
P/N	promissory note 本票
P. O.	purchase order 订购单
POD	port of discharge 卸货港
POE	port of entry 报关港口
POL	port of loading 装货港
PTO	please tum overleaf 请阅后页
P. S.	postscript 附言

Q

Qty	quantity 数量
Quotn.	quotation 报价
QC	quality control 质量控制

R

Ref.	reference 参考；关于
RF	reefer container 冷藏集装箱
Ro-Ro Ship	roll-on roll-off ship 滚装船
R/T	revenue rons 计费吨
R & T	rail and truck 铁路及卡车运输
R & W	rail and water 铁路及水路运输

S

SAFE	State Administration of Foreign Exchange 国家外汇管理局
SAMR	(China) State Administration for Market Regulation (中国) 国家市场监督管理总局
SAR	Special Administrative Region 特别行政区
SAT	(China) State Administration of Taxation (中国) 国家税务总局
S/C	sales confirmation 销售确认书
SEC	special economic zone 经济特区
SITC	Standard International Trade Classification 国际贸易标准分类
SLC	standby LC 备用信用证

SMEs   small and medium-sized enterprises 中小型企业

S/O   shipping order 装船单；下货纸；关单

SOE   state-owned enterprises 国有企业

Spec.   specification 规格；尺寸

S. R. C. C.   strike, riots and civil commotions 罢工、暴力、民变险

S/S；S. S.   steamship 轮船

Sq.   square 平方；结清

SWIFT   Society for Worldwide Inter Bank Financial Telecommunications 全球
               银行间金融电讯协会

T

TEU   twenty-foot equivalent unit 20 英尺标准集装箱计算单位

T. H. C   terminal handling charge 码头操作费

T. R. S   terminal receiving station 码头收货站

TST   test 检查，检测

T/T   telegraphic transfer 电汇

TV   terminal value 最终价值

TW   transit warehouse 转口仓库

T. O. P.   turn over, please 请翻转

TPND   Theft, Pilferage, and Non-delivery 偷窃、提货不着险

TQC   total quality control 全面质量控制

T/R   trust Receipt 信托收据

U

UBR   uniform business rate 统一商业税率

UBS   Union Bank of Switzerland 瑞士联合银行

UCP   Uniform Customs and Practice for Documentary Credits 跟单信用证统
               一惯例

UOS   unless otherwise stated 除非另有规定

URC   Uniform Rules for Collections 托收统一规则

V

V. A. T.   value added tax 增值税

Via.   through, by way of 经由；通过

VIP   very important person 贵宾

Vol.   volume 量；容积

Voy.   voyage 航次

VOC	vendor quality certification 售主质量确认
VQA	vendor quality assurance 售主质量保证
VS	versus 对于
VSQ	very special quality 特级质量

W

W. P. A.	With Particular Average/With Average 水渍险
W. R.	War Risks 战争险
WT	weight 重量
WTO	World Trade Organization 世界贸易组织
W/W	warehouse to warehouse 仓至仓
WWW	Worldwide Web 万维网；全球计算机网

References

参考文献

[1] 薄如翾.外贸电邮营销实战[M].北京:中国海关出版社, 2017.

[2] 陈振东.新编外贸英语函电写作教程[M].北京:对外经济贸易大学出版社, 2015.

[3] 邓志新.国际贸易实务[M].北京:人民邮电出版社, 2021.

[4] 丁婷, 王若梅, 冯军, 等.跨境电商函电与商务写作[M].北京:中国海关出版社, 2018.

[5] 浩瀚, 陈淑萍.商务英语写作实战案例[M].北京:北京航空航天大学出版社, 2011.

[6] 刘裕.巧用外贸邮件拿订单[M].北京:中国海关出版社, 2013.

[7] 时敏, 兰天.外贸英语函电[M].北京:科学出版社, 2016.

[8] 尹小莹, 范晶晶.外贸英语函电[M].西安:西安交通大学出版社, 2019.

[9] 毅冰.外贸高手客户成交技巧[M].北京:中国海关出版社, 2014.

[10] 毅冰.十天搞定外贸函电[M].北京:中国海关出版社, 2014.

[11] 赵银德.外贸函电[M].北京:机械工业出版社, 2016.

ZHEJIANG UNIVERSITY PRESS
浙江大学出版社

互联网+教育+出版

立方书

教育信息化趋势下，课堂教学的创新催生教材的创新，互联网+教育的融合创新，教材呈现全新的表现形式——教材即课堂。

轻松备课　分享资源　发送通知　作业评测　互动讨论

"一本书"带来"一个课堂"　教学改革从"扫一扫"开始

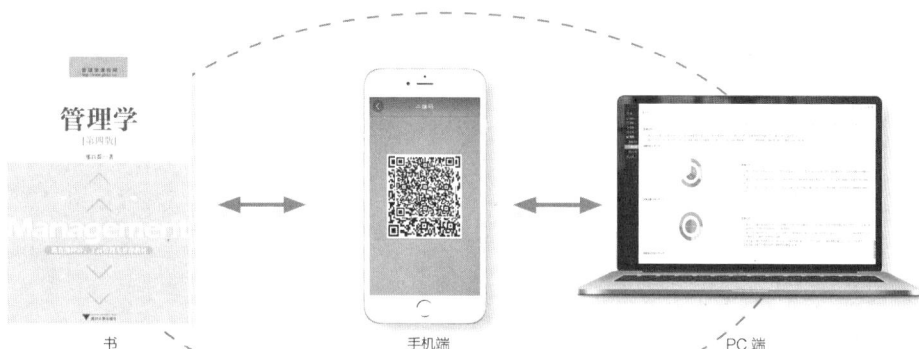

管理学

书　　　　　　　　手机端　　　　　　　　PC 端

打造中国大学课堂新模式

【创新的教学体验】

开课教师可免费申请"立方书"开课，利用本书配套的资源及自己上传的资源进行教学。

【方便的班级管理】

教师可以轻松创建、管理自己的课堂，后台控制简便，可视化操作，一体化管理。

【完善的教学功能】

课程模块、资源内容随心排列，备课、开课，管理学生、发送通知、分享资源、布置和批改作业、组织讨论答疑、开展教学互动。

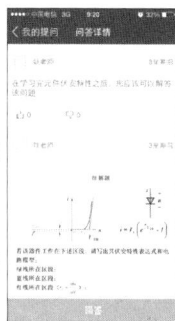

扫一扫 下载APP

教师开课流程

在APP内扫描封面二维码，申请资源

开通教师权限，登录网站

创建课堂，生成课堂二维码

学生扫码加入课堂，轻松上课

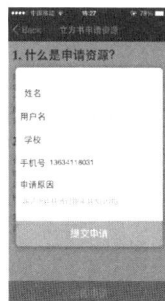

网站地址：www.lifangshu.com
技术支持：lifangshu2015@126.com；电话：0571-88273329